# The Challenge of Old Testament Women 2

# The Challenge of Old Testament Women 2

A Guide for Bible Study Groups

## Sara Buswell

## BAKER BOOK HOUSE
Grand Rapids, Michigan 49516

ISBN: 0-8010-0932-4

*Second printing, January 1989*

Scripture quotations, unless otherwise indicated,
are taken from the New International Version.
Copyright 1973, 1978, 1984 by New York International Bible Society.
Used with permission of Zondervan Bible Publishers.

Printed in the United States of America

Cover art: Gerrit van Honthorst, Dutch.
*Samson and Delilah,* oil
The Cleveland Museum of Art,
Mr. and Mrs. William H. Marlatt Fund.
Used with permission.

In depicting this scene, Honthorst has taken some liberties with the Old
Testament account which mentions only a male accomplice who performed
the actual shaving of Samson's head.

For
Jamie,
for always


"Not by might, nor by power, but
by my Spirit," says the LORD Almighty.
Zechariah 4:6

# Contents

PART THREE

## Women of Seduction    105

PART FOUR

## Women of Hospitality and Service    145

# Introduction

From the title of this book, you have probably guessed that this is the second series of studies on women of the Old Testament. "And what will you write next?" is the well-meaning question I hear now. "Will it be 'New Testament Women,' or maybe 'Old Testament Men'?"

The intent is to encourage, I believe, yet there is in the question a hidden suggestion that surely now, after *two* books, I must be through with the subject at last, or at least nearly out of material. But I'm not, and I hope that you are not, either, because God still would teach us more if we would continue to search carefully in his Word and apply his principles faithfully to our lives today.

Most of the more familiar names have been used, or at least considered, in these first two volumes. But perhaps for you the real treasure still lies ahead, as you dig deeper, for yourself, in territory yet uncharted. We may not recognize the names, and we may have more difficulty finding the texts, but they are there: Shiphrah and Puah, the wise woman of Tekoa, Jael, Hephzibah, the lady at Abel-beth-maacah, the woman with the jars of oil, Jezebel, the mother of the child Solomon offered to divide in half, Noah's wife, Athaliah, Gomer, Dinah, the witch of Endor, Jemima, Jephthah's daughter, the perfect woman in Proverbs 31, and many others. Who would dare to claim that these women are unimportant simply because they were not included in these two studies? Rather, I think it must be the other way around.

There is always more to discover in God's living Word, even within a narrow range of study. As you continue on your own or with a group of friends, remember the guidelines and the purpose of your search as we have begun it together. Don't water down the Scriptures or weaken the punch of its message. Let each woman speak from within her own context. With prayer and imagination, put yourself in her situation, and invite God to reveal and apply his relevant principles to your life through her story. Don't indulge in fantasy. Fake jewels have no value, however attractive they may be. The Bible is true, its characters real historical people just as we are. What a privilege we have to know our God, and ourselves, through its study and application. The challenge continues. I pray you will enjoy it and share it as you grow.

Sara Buswell

# Study Plan

1. Read the questions at the beginning of each lesson.
2. Read the Scripture passage(s) listed and be aware of the questions as you read. Allow time to think about words or phrases or incidents that are especially meaningful to you. Underline them in your Bible.
3. Formulate initial answer(s) to questions.
4. If possible, discuss answers with a friend or group.
5. Read the lesson commentary.
6. Revise answers, if necessary.
7. Apply your answers to your life as God directs.

# PART ONE

# Women of Faith

Hannah

Shunammite Woman

Jochebed

We have all had mothers and many of us are mothers. Volumes of research have analyzed the behaviors and influences of mothers, especially in the last one hundred years. Motherhood is a domain with which we all feel experienced in various ways. Because we carry a set of expectations of what normal motherly behavior is, our attention is aroused and we become curious to discover some explanation when a particular mother behaves in an unusual manner toward her children.

The definition of faith in Hebrews 11:1 tells us at once that something unusual is at work: "Now faith is being sure of what we hope for, and certain of what we do not see." The passage continues with a remarkable chronicle of saints—Abel, Enoch, Noah, Abraham, Isaac, Jacob, Moses, and others. Every person in this "great cloud of witnesses" proved his or her profound faith by displaying unshakable confidence that God would indeed fulfill his promises, despite outward appearances or normal expectations to the contrary and despite the fact that these saints did not receive what had been promised them during their lifetimes.

In selecting three mothers from the Bible to portray faith, I am not suggesting that mothers are the only beings who live or act in this way. What is interesting is the fact that Hannah, Jochebed, and the Shunammite woman all exemplified faith through their unusual actions and attitudes as mothers, in contrast to what we might consider normal responses to their circumstances. Their reward was that God answered their prayers and included their stories in his Word to move and challenge us to be women of faith today.

# 1
## Hannah

### Primary Scripture Reading

1 Samuel 1, 2

### Supplementary References

Numbers 6:1–21
Psalm 84:3

### Questions for Study and Discussion

**1.** Describe Hannah's household. What was her relationship with Elkanah? Who was Peninnah? How did Elkanah and Peninnah either encourage or provoke Hannah? For how long?

**2.** When and why was Hannah most unhappy? What did she do about her deep sorrow? How did the priest Eli respond to her behavior in 1 Samuel 1:10–18? When did Hannah stop praying? Why? What impresses you most about this passage?

**3.** Read Numbers 6:1–21. What are the requirements and purposes of a Nazirite vow? Was Hannah trying to bargain with God, or was she proving her expectant faith by her vow? Have you ever made a vow to God? Could you tell about the circumstances and the results?

**4.** Why did Hannah name her baby Samuel? What do you think about her actions in 1 Samuel 1:21–28? What was the hardest moment in her commitment? From what you know of Eli's and Samuel's later history, as well as from these early chapters of the book, would you admire or criticize Hannah for leaving her son at the house of the Lord?

**5.** What attributes of God are mentioned in Hannah's prayer (1 Sam. 2:1–10)? In what ways are humans to respond to God, according to these verses? What connection do you find between the content of Hannah's prayer and the circumstances of her life at this time?

**6.** Compare Hannah's action in bringing Samuel to the house of the Lord with the attitude expressed in Psalm 84:3. As a parent, how could you fully commit your offspring to God and still fulfill your responsibility to raise them? What was unique about Hannah's performance of her role as a mother that demonstrates her strong faith?

**7.** In which ways was Hannah blessed by God for her faith? How does her example encourage your faith in God in your difficult circumstances today?

H annah was barren in an age in which conception of children was perceived to be a sign of God's blessing as well as being a practical protection of one's future rights and property. Not long after Hannah's time, Solomon wrote, "Sons are a heritage from the LORD, children a reward from him. Like arrows in the hands of a warrior are sons born in one's youth. Blessed is the man whose quiver is full of them" (Ps. 127:5). On the other hand, a lack of offspring was viewed not only as a serious threat to one's security but also as a direct punishment from the Lord. Vestiges of the same feelings and societal expectations remain today.

Hannah's failure to provide offspring was even more painful because her husband Elkanah had another wife, Peninnah, who would not let her forget the fact for a moment.

> Peninnah had children, but Hannah had none. Year after year this man [Elkanah] went up from his town to worship and sacrifice to the LORD Almighty at Shiloh, where Hophni and Phinehas, the two sons of Eli, were priests of the LORD. Whenever the day came for Elkanah to sacrifice, he would give portions of the meat to his wife Peninnah and to all her sons and daughters. But to Hannah he gave a double portion because he loved her, and the LORD had closed her womb. And because the LORD had closed her womb, her rival kept provoking her in order to irritate her. This went on year after year. Whenever Hannah went up to the house of the LORD, her rival provoked her till she wept and would not eat (1 Sam. 1:2–7).

Elkanah was aware of Peninnah's constant cruelty, and he tried to do something about it by saying to Hannah, "Hannah, why are you weeping? Why don't you eat? Why are you downhearted? Don't I mean more to you than ten sons?" (1 Sam. 1:8). He was probably just trying to be helpful, but Elkanah was not very sensitive. At best we can read his questions as a magnanimous gesture of comfort and a further demonstration of his sincere love for Hannah (in addition to his provision of a double portion of meat at the sacrifice, v. 5). At worst they may sound rather self-centered and unsympathetic. In either

19

case, his questions failed to penetrate to the real problem or to point the way to a solution.

## Prayer

It does not appear that Hannah had sought Elkanah's help or comfort, nor did she seem annoyed at his conceit. There was a solution to her problem, Hannah knew, but it did not begin with her husband. Instead,

> In bitterness of soul Hannah wept much and prayed to the LORD. And she made a vow, saying, "O LORD Almighty, if you will only look upon your servant's misery and remember me, and not forget your servant but give her a son, then I will give him to the LORD for all the days of his life, and no razor will ever be used on his head" (1 Sam. 1:10–11).

Over the next several verses, we are reminded of her intensity: "She kept on praying" (v. 12); "Hannah was praying in her heart" (v. 13); and, "I was pouring out my soul to the LORD. . . . I have been praying here out of my great anguish and grief" (vs. 15–16). Here, then, is the first indication of Hannah's faith. She took her deep troubles directly to God, trusting that he could, while others could not, provide a way of release from her distress.

Right now you, too, can choose to follow her example, and in the words of David, "Cast thy burden upon the LORD, and he shall sustain thee: he shall never suffer the righteous to be moved" (Ps. 55:22, KJV).

## Promise

The actual content of Hannah's prayer deserves our careful attention. It followed the prescribed pattern of a Nazirite vow, which was ordained by God in Numbers 6:1–21:

> If a man or woman wants to make a special vow, a vow of separation to the LORD as a Nazirite, he must abstain from wine and other fermented drink and must not drink vinegar made from wine or from other fermented drink. He must not drink grape juice or eat grapes or raisins. As long as he is a Nazirite, he must not eat anything that comes from the grapevine, not even the seeds or skins. During the entire period of his vow of separation no razor may be used on his head. He must be holy until the period of his separation to the LORD is over; he must let the hair of his head grow long. Throughout the period of his separation to the LORD he must not go near a dead body. . . . Throughout the period of his separation he is consecrated to the LORD. . . . This is the law of the Nazirite who vows his offering to the LORD in accordance with his separation, . . . He must fulfill the vow he has made, according to the law of the Nazirite.

This kind of vow represented a special provision by which a man or woman could consecrate himself or herself wholly to God for a specific purpose and for a limited period of time. After the conditions were fulfilled, careful instructions prescribed hair-shaving and sacrifices to signify God's acceptance of the vow and release from its constraints. In addition, any contact with a dead body while under vow constituted defilement, which necessitated total rededication of the vow. This meant recleansing, sacrificing, and starting the period of consecration over again. Finally, a person making such a vow was required to abstain from cutting the hair and from drinking wine. In short, the Nazirite vow was a serious transaction with the Lord; it represented a personal decision to become a "fragrant offering, an acceptable sacrifice, pleasing to God" (Phil. 4:18).

Critics have accused Hannah of wrongfully trying to bargain with God, because of the if—then clause in her promise. But rather than driving a bargain or trying to manipulate God, Hannah was dedicating herself wholly to him in faith by promising to return to his service the child whom she already believed he would provide. Keeping her end of the promise by sealing her commitment with a vow was a further important step in her journey of faith.

In the New Testament, Paul appears to have taken part in similar vows (Acts 18:18, 21:23–26). In John 15:19 and elsewhere, Jesus reminds us that he has chosen his own to be set apart, in the world but not of the world, for his service. How serious is your commitment to him?

The Nazirite vow was almost always initiated by an individual on his own behalf and for a limited period. But Hannah's vow consecrated her son to the Lord from the first anticipation of his conception through his entire lifetime. Samson and John the Baptist are the only other biblical examples of Nazirite vows pledged by parents (Judg. 13:5; Luke 1:15). In both cases, the command to consecrate these children was delivered by angels. What extraordinary commitment *by faith* shines through the mothers of each of these men!

## Peace

Hannah was persistent and completely honest in expressing her desperate desire for a son. She did not leave her prayers until she felt sure that God had heard and would answer them. How do we know she received this assurance? When she finished her conversation with the priest Eli, who had observed and misunderstood the significance of her vow, he blessed her. "Eli answered, 'Go in peace, and may the God of Israel grant you what you have asked of him.' She said, 'May your servant find favor in your eyes.' *Then she went her way and ate something, and her face was no longer downcast*" (1 Sam. 1:17, 18, italics added).

Here is the second mark of Hannah's faith. This turnabout of countenance was possible only because of her determination to *believe* that God *would* answer her need. She had not yet become pregnant, but she could eat and be cheerful *in faith*. Over and over again the psalms also express this same kind of radiant confidence in God: "In the day of my trouble I will call to you: for you will answer me" (Ps. 86:7; see also Pss. 56:3–4, 91:2, 138:7).

Do you exercise this determination to trust in God's help even before you see the end product? Throughout his Word, God continually invites us to *test* his promises in faith, so that we can praise him when he overwhelms us with his blessings.

This poor man called, and the LORD heard him; he saved him out of all his troubles. The angel of the LORD encamps around those who fear him, and he delivers them. Taste and see that the LORD is good; blessed is the man who takes refuge in him (Ps. 34:6–8).

"Bring the whole tithe into the storehouse, that there may be food in my house. Test me in this," says the LORD Almighty, "and see if I will not throw open the floodgates of heaven and pour out so much blessing that you will not have room enough for it" (Mal. 3:10).

There is a note of warning here, as well. To test God with an attitude of unbelief—an expectation that he must perform at our command or for our convenience—is strictly forbidden (see Deut. 6:16; Matt. 4:7). The difference between the right and wrong kind of testing lies both in the attitude of the asker and in the results of prayer. Hannah's heart was right toward God, and he blessed her. We would do well to examine our own motives before we come to him in prayer.

The peace that Hannah evidenced in her restored appetite and appearance following Eli's blessing of her vow lasted until her son was born, and is reflected in the name she chose for him. "So in the course of time Hannah conceived and gave birth to a son. She named him Samuel, saying, 'Because I asked the LORD for him'" (1 Sam. 1:20). The name Samuel sounds like the Hebrew word for *heard of God.* In naming her son, Hannah honored the Lord for hearing and answering her prayers. Here is another lesson in faith for us. In addition to believing that God would do what she had asked, she did not forget to praise him for hearing her prayers.

God delights in giving his children the desires of their hearts. And, like any parent, he likes to be appreciated. When Jesus healed ten lepers, only one returned to thank him.

> Jesus asked, "Were not all ten cleansed? Where are the other nine? Was no one found to return and give praise to God except this foreigner?" Then he said to him "Rise and go, your faith has made you well" (Luke 17:17–19).

Hannah's expression of thankfulness was a further demonstration of the peace she experienced within.

## Praise

Once Hannah had made her vow she was no longer sad, but she had yet to fulfill her vow. In one sense, having made the solemn commitment, she had set a determined course to dedicate her son, and therefore may have gained strength through discipline to carry it to completion. "Once begun is half done" is a familiar adage. However, we know from our own experience that it is often much harder to *do* a thing than simply talk about it (like losing weight or reforming a bad habit). The remainder of 1 Samuel 1 and 2 allows us to glimpse Hannah at critical moments: she conceived, gave birth, refused to go to Shiloh until Samuel was weaned, brought him to the house of the Lord and entrusted him to Eli, and brought her son a new coat each year when she visited him. Did she show any signs of regret or

25

wavering in her self-assigned promise? Nothing but joy radiates through this scene of her bringing Samuel to Eli:

> After he was weaned, she took the boy with her, young as he was, along with a three-year-old bull, an ephah of flour and a skin of wine, and brought him to the house of the LORD at Shiloh. When they had slaughtered the bull, they brought the boy to Eli, and she said to him, "As surely as you live, my lord, I am the woman who stood here beside you praying to the LORD, I prayed for this child, and the LORD has granted me what I asked of him. So now I give him to the LORD. For his whole life he will be given over to the LORD." And he worshiped the LORD there (1 Sam. 1:24–28).

In addition to these details, Hannah's beautiful psalm of praise is also recorded for us:

> Then Hannah prayed and said:
> "My heart rejoices in the LORD;
>     in the LORD my horn is lifted high.
> My mouth boasts over my enemies,
>     for I delight in your deliverance.
>
> "There is no one holy like the LORD;
>     there is no one besides you;
>     there is no Rock like our God.
>
> "Do not keep talking so proudly
>     or let your mouth speak such arrogance,
> for the LORD is a God who knows,
>     and by him deeds are weighed.

"The bows of the warriors are broken,
but those who stumbled are armed with strength.
Those who were full hire themselves out for food,
but those who were hungry hunger no more.
She who was barren has borne seven children,
but she who has had many sons pines away.

"The LORD brings death and makes alive;
he brings down to the grave and raises up.
The LORD sends poverty and wealth;
he humbles and he exalts.

He raises the poor from the dust
and lifts the needy from the ash heap;
he seats them with princes
and has them inherit a throne of honor.

"For the foundations of the earth are the LORD's;
upon them he has set the world.
He will guard the feet of his saints,
but the wicked will be silenced in darkness.

"It is not by strength that one prevails;
those who oppose the LORD will be shattered.
He will thunder against them from heaven;
the LORD will judge the ends of the earth.

Many authors have pointed out similarities between this prayer and Mary's psalm of praise at the Annunciation (compare Luke 1:46–55).

What was it that enabled Hannah to fulfill her promise with such poise and praise, rather than anxiety and mourning over having to part from the child she had desired for so long? There is only one explanation. Her deep, living faith gave Hannah the assurance that God had heard and answered her prayers, and that he was fully able to protect, guide, and use Samuel for his glory. Although some people have criticized this mother for abandoning her young child to the influence of the old priest and his wicked sons (Eli's bad example is sometimes blamed for Samuel's later difficulties with his own sons—see 1 Sam. 8:1–5), I view her action and her attitude as evidence of her solid conviction that she was actually entrusting Samuel to the Lord himself, who could oversee and overrule in every human situation.

## Provision

Hannah made and kept her promise to God in faith. Every year she made a coat for Samuel and brought it to him when she visited him at Shiloh (1 Sam. 2:19). She did not try to forget about this child whom she had given to the Lord. Rather, she continued to provide what she could for him while he served in the better place appointed by God for him. We also want to see that God kept his promises to Hannah throughout this beautiful story. The Nazirite vow seemed to be initiated by Hannah, but God honored his part of the commitment and added further blessings to her request. Every year Eli prayed for Elkanah and his wife, saying,

> "May the LORD give you children by this woman to take the place of the one she prayed for and gave to the LORD." Then they would go home. And the LORD was gracious to Hannah; she conceived and gave birth to three sons and two daughters. Meanwhile, the boy

Samuel grew up in the presence of the Lord (1 Sam. 2:20–21).

God did more for Hannah than simply provide a son who would be returned to his own service. He gave her peace and purpose and greater productivity than she had any reason to expect. And he kept Samuel in his presence. Surely he is worthy of the feeble responses we make to his abundant blessings.

Not every mother is asked to dedicate her child to fulltime Christian ministry, nor should it be so. But we are asked to give our children fully into God's care for whatever particular purpose he has designed, and to dedicate them joyfully to it, whatever the distance or cost. Even if we have no physical offspring, we can dedicate ourselves wholeheartedly as children of God. Indeed, such total commitment is a privilege, and it brings blessing (2 Chron. 16:9).

Hannah's faith ministered to me several years ago when, much to my surprise, I found myself in tears on the night before my son's first day of kindergarten. Even though I had thought I was looking forward to that day for many months, and though I had prepared him for it with anticipation of new clothes, friends, and adventures, I discovered I was obviously still unwilling to deposit him irrevocably on that doorstep of independence and learning known as school. Then I was moved to remember Hannah's example. She never showed such ambivalence. She had cherished all along the thought that I only recalled in the morning: God would *always* be with her son, even where and when she could not go with him. I imagined that she prayed constantly for her

29

little boy while they were separated, and I could and would do the same for mine.

Soon after my experience I discovered another verse which I frequently claim as a reminder to myself that my children are always more secure in God's hands than in mine: "Yea, the sparrow hath found an house, and the swallow a nest for herself, where she may lay her young, even thine altars, O LORD of hosts, my King, and my God" (Ps. 84:3, KJV).

Knowing this truth, what better option could Hannah choose than to entrust her son to God in his house and rejoice? Do you share her joy, so that you, too, wholeheartedly entrust your family and future to him?

# 2

## Shunammite Woman

### Primary Scripture Reading

2 Kings 4 and 8

### Supplementary References

Luke 4:14, 15
Philippians 3:12–14
Hebrews 4:15, 16

### Questions for Study and Discussion

**1.** What was the situation of the Shunammite woman? What did she do for Elisha? Did she have an ulterior motive for her action, do you think?

**2.** What did Elisha offer to do for her? How did she respond? What emotions underlay her reaction?

**3.** What assumptions was Gehazi making in 2 Kings 4:14? Why did the Shunammite protest in 4:16? What did she mean when she quoted herself in 4:28?

**4.** List the full sequence of events following the boy's death. Why was the Shunammite evasive toward her husband and Gehazi? Did she deliberately lie to them? What differences do you observe between those two men and Elisha?

**5.** Find the approximate distance from Shunem to Mount Carmel. At what point in her journey would you say the woman's faith and patience were most sorely tried? Why?

**6.** How was the Shunammite rewarded for her persistent faith in 2 Kings 4? How in 2 Kings 8? Have you experienced either kind of miracle? In what ways have you been persistent? How can you use the Shunammite's story to activate your faith?

**7.** If a true prophet of God offered to perform some service for you, what would you ask for? What is keeping you from expressing your heart's desire to God himself right now? Spend a few moments in honest, expectant prayer.

Throughout his ministry, the prophet Elisha exercised tremendous power and authority from God to prophesy and perform miracles. Among the many individuals to whom he ministered, the well-to-do woman of Shunem stands out as a beautiful testimony to dynamic faith. This unnamed woman's preparation and persistence enabled her to experience God's providential power in a unique way. Her perception of God's character and personality challenge us to expect God to meet our needs when we place our faith wholly in him.

### Preparation

The Shunammite's preparation for Elisha provides the first evidence of her faith. In 2 Kings 4:8, she began by urging him to stay for one meal. Her hospitality must have been both gracious and delicious; Elisha readily became a regular guest whenever he came by. Soon the woman proposed to her husband that they build a special room for Elisha, explaining, "I know that this man who often comes our way is a holy man of God" (2 Kings 4:9).

The fact that the woman recognized Elisha as a prophet suggests both his considerable reputation and her own ready faith. Her motive was genuine. Although she was well aware of the stature of her guest, she offered him her hospitality in service to God and not as a means of obtaining any credit or recognition for herself. There is no hint of her boasting or gossiping to friends about her famous guest, or appealing to him for special favors. For his part, Elisha obviously appreciated both the meals and the restful haven she provided in her home. His offer to render some service to her (2 Kings 4:13) derived in turn from his sincere gratitude, not from any sense of obligation.

In considering the quality of the Shunammite's preparation, will you first examine your own motives? Is your hospitality offered in service to God only, or do you secretly hope to gain some other direct or indirect benefit from it? Jesus warned:

> "When you give a luncheon or dinner, do not invite your friends, your brothers or relatives, or your rich neighbors; if you do, they may invite you back and so you will be repaid. But when you give a banquet, invite the poor, the crippled, the lame, the blind, and you will be blessed. Although they cannot repay you, you will be repaid at the resurrection of the righteous" (Luke 14:12–15).

It is interesting to notice Elisha's offer of service to the Shunammite: "Can we speak on your behalf to the king or the commander of the army?" (2 Kings 4:13). He did not propose petitioning God in her behalf, even though his primary renown and duty were as a prophet and not as a royal or military confidant. Why did he limit his offer to the national rather than the spiritual realm, especially since the real desire of her heart (to have a child) could only be granted by God? Clearly, she recognized who he was; so he could not have been trying to conceal his identity or power. Could he have been evaluating her motives and her faith by giving her an opportunity to express her deep desire and to turn to God for help without Elisha's prompting? If so, did she fail or pass the test?

### Prophecy

Without our knowing exactly what Elisha had in mind with his question, it is not easy to interpret the Shunammite's reply: "I have a home among my own people" (2 Kings 4:13). Why did she not simply tell Elisha of her deep longing for a child? Several reasons are suggested below, with some possible hidden attitudes in parentheses:

1. To have "a home among her own people" was fully satisfying to her. Her family's support had helped her withstand the prejudice of her culture against the childless. (Contentment, security)
2. She wanted a child, but she did not mention her desire because Elisha had only offered to speak to the king or commander, neither of whom could have helped in her situation. (Realism)

34

3. She wanted a child, but she did not feel that her own gesture of hospitality was sufficient to merit such a large blessing in return. She did not wish to bother the great prophet with her problems. (Humility)
4. She wanted a child, but she did not really believe that Elisha or even God himself had the power to grant her desire. (Doubt, lack of faith)
5. She wanted a child, but she felt that her barrenness was a judgment or punishment from God (in accordance with the beliefs of her culture), which even Elisha could not overturn. (Shame, disgrace)
6. She wanted a child, but she would not expose her private longing to further derision or disappointment. (Pride)
7. She accepted her childlessness as God's plan for her, so she was no longer "kicking against the goads"; this unmet desire was no longer a burning issue that needed to be brought up. (Peace)

Why did the Shunammite answer Elisha as she did? It is impossible to say with certainty which of the above explanations, or any others you may wish to offer, most accurately represent the true state of the Shunammite's feelings. Probably a combination of desires and fears was at work to keep her from talking freely with God's prophet about her yearning for a child.

It is well worth considering how we might respond to such an offer of assistance as Elisha made, and what underlying attitudes may be reflected in the thoughts we either express aloud or keep hidden within our hearts. Are we afraid to tell the Lord our innermost fears and hopes? He knows them all, whether we confess them or not. Do we trust him to deal gently and wisely with our very souls?

> For we do not have a high priest who is unable to sympathize with our weaknesses, but we have one who has been tempted in every way, just as we are— yet was without sin. Let us then approach the throne of grace with confidence, so that we may receive mercy and find grace to help us in our time of need (Heb. 4:15–16).

Although the Shunammite did not express it openly, it did not take long for Elisha, through his servant Gehazi, to discern her true desire: "Well, she has no son and her husband is old" (2 Kings 4:14). The almost desperate tone in her response to the prophet's promise of a son within the year proved the accuracy of Gehazi's perception. She protested, "No, my lord. Don't mislead your servant, O man of God!" (2 Kings 4:16). It is evident that her hesitation was only founded in the fear that Elisha's promise might not come to pass. Indeed, Elisha had prophesied the very event that she had desired most but had given up all hope of attaining.

### Persistence

All went well for a few years. The Shunammite conceived and gave birth to a son the following year, as Elisha had foretold. We can readily imagine her boundless joy and praise to God for his unexpected blessing. But one morning, when the boy went out to his father in the fields, he suddenly cried out, "My head! My head!"

and collapsed. He was carried to his mother's lap, where he sat until noon and then died. The mother's reaction is quite remarkable: no screams, no calls for help, no tears, no rending of clothes, nor even any effort to revive the child. Instead, "she went up and laid him on the bed of the man of God, then shut the door and went out" (2 Kings 4:21). As far as she was concerned, the boy's death was unacceptable; therefore, she refused to acknowledge it with any outward sign, either of panic or of mourning.

When tragedy strikes in our lives, isn't it a normal reaction to deny its existence, to shout out, "No! It isn't true!" and to try to erase the facts by the very volume of our cries? It requires all of our faith to accept such trials and at the same time claim and receive the full comfort of God's love in the midst of our grief. Then, especially, we must cling tightly to what we know of his character and his care, trusting his plan to be perfect even when we least understand it.

The Shunammite's crisis both strained and strengthened her faith. It drew her into a closer relationship with God, not through passive acceptance but through action. She was so certain that the Lord would not have promised and then provided a son, only to take him from her so soon, that she quietly laid him on the prophet's bed and set out to secure the only power that could effectively help in her situation. She understood that only God *could* restore her son, and she believed that he *would*. She had no need to tell God what to do, but, knowing what he would do, she acted forthrightly to claim the full amount of his blessing for her.

The rapid flow of events that followed the boy's death is a wonderful demonstration of faith in action. There was not a moment's indecision or delay. No time or word was wasted. No obstacle or distraction could sway her from her goal, which was to fetch Elisha to the bedroom she had provided for him, in order that he might restore her child to life.

Consider the individuals who in some way cluttered her path but were dispatched by her urgent authority.

| Person | Obstruction (question/action) | Her Response |
|---|---|---|
| *Husband* | "Why go to him today? It's not the New Moon or the Sabbath." | "It's all right." |
| *Servant/ Donkey* | | *She* saddled the donkey and said to her servant, "Don't slow down for me unless I tell you." |
| *Gehazi* | (Sent by Elisha to ask whether everything was all right) | "Everything is all right." |
| | Came over to push her away | Took hold of Elisha's feet |
| *Elisha* | But the man of God said, "Leave her alone! She is in bitter distress, but the LORD has hidden it from me and has not told me why." (Sent Gehazi with his staff to lay it on the boy's face) So he got up and followed her. | "Did I ask you for a son, my lord?" she said. "Didn't I tell you, 'Don't raise my hopes'?"  "As surely as the LORD lives and as you live, I will not leave you." |

Many of us would say that we are sincerely seeking God's will for our lives, yet how casually we sometimes amble toward the goals his will prescribes. Do we know the difference between a goal and an obstacle? We must learn from the Shunammite's example to pursue God's promises with urgent confidence, letting no person or circumstance hinder our attainment of every glory for his name's sake. The apostle Paul adds the spiritual as well as the practical aspect of this quest.

> Not that I have already obtained all this, or have already been made perfect, but I press on to take hold of that for which Christ Jesus took hold of me. Brothers, I do not consider myself yet to have taken hold of it. But one thing I do: Forgetting what is behind and straining toward what is ahead, I press on toward the goal to win the prize for which God has called me heavenward in Christ Jesus (Phil. 3:12–14).

Nothing should be permitted to dissuade, distract, or discourage us from obtaining this prize for ourselves. In spite of our present trials, we must realize the power and personality of God as well as the Shunammite woman did, so that we, too, may set our feet on course to attain the full measure of his promise. We must choose to know him better, through study and application of his Word, so that our lives may radiate such persistent faith as the Shunammite demonstrated.

Two other observations may be made from the chart above. First, the husband's objection, "Why go to him today? It's not the New Moon or the Sabbath" (2 Kings 4:23) reveals that his concept of seeking the Lord was limited to outward forms or ritual observances. He did not need God except in the performance of his religious obligations (compare Col. 2:16). His wife was quite different. She knew God more personally, through his servant Elisha, and she understood immediately that he alone could help in her desperate emergency. She sought God out of critical need, not ritual requirement, and he responded out of love.

Why do you worship? Do you attend church on Sundays because you feel you are supposed to? Or do you seek God's presence at all times because you must, since only he can "satisfy the desires of every living thing" (Ps. 145:16)?

The second point to notice is the nature and necessity of the Shunammite woman's journey. Why did she travel so far (about sixty miles for the round trip) and so fast (she left after the child died at noon, and presumably returned with Elisha before nightfall), when she could have asked the Lord directly to save her son?

To answer, we must keep in mind the historical setting of this story. In the age of the Old Testament prophets, God's power was manifest primarily through his particular appointed servants, who proclaimed his word and performed miracles in his name. This does not mean that God was ever inaccessible or indifferent to the needs or calls of any individual who turned to him for help. The Shunammite was aware and appreciative of God's personal interest in her family, and she responded personally to his promise of a child. Still, she was not able to experience the same kind of intimate relationship with the Lord that believers can enjoy today through the Holy Spirit. For her, Elisha represented God in word and

40

deed, and she was convinced that only by bringing him physically to her child could she avail herself of God's power. Apparently, she was correct in her conclusion, since neither Elisha's servant nor his wooden staff sent in his absence had any effect on the boy. In fact, the woman's perceptions were even clearer than those of Elisha himself, who had to admit that the reason for her distress was at first hidden from him (2 Kings 4:27). He submitted to her demands because it was evident that she knew better than he what and how God would work in her situation. With our privilege of direct access to God through Christ when we pray today, we dare not become so complacent that we fail to avail ourselves of every comfort, guidance, and power he extends.

## Preparation, Persistence, and Provision Repeated

In 2 Kings 8, we find a beautiful sequel to the Shunammite's story. Again we see her preparation as she obeyed Elisha's instructions to "go away with your family and stay wherever you can, because the LORD has decreed a famine in the land that will last seven years" (2 Kings 8:1). When she returned, she discovered that her house and land had been confiscated. Again we see her persistence in coming directly to the king to beg for the restoration of her property. And again we see God's perfect provision for her.

Obedience is the outward expression of inner faith. The Shunammite who had already experienced first God's promise through the prophet of a child and then his power to restore the child to life, did not hesitate to

41

believe Elisha's prediction of famine and to obey his command to leave the country. The simple statement, "The woman proceeded to do as the man of God said" (2 Kings 8:2), is in marked contrast to her earlier protest: "No, my lord. Don't mislead your servant, O man of God!" (2 Kings 4:16), and demonstrates her growing faith. Of course, the nature of the second prophecy was quite different from the first one; instead of touching her deepest personal desire, the famine was a more general and external pronouncement of God's judgment against the entire nation. Even so, we can sense a change in her attitude—greater regard for Elisha and deeper reverence for God—which grew out of her previous experiences. It had not been wrong for her to question Elisha on the earlier occasion, but her subsequent experience and faith were such that she did not need to question him any further. She simply obeyed. In what ways have your faith and experience in the past prepared you to accept and obey God's present commands to you?

Seven years elapsed, and the famine ended. The Shunammite, apparently a widow by this time, displayed the same clear perception of her need, the same assessment of resources, and the same decisiveness we observed in 2 Kings 4. As we saw her thrust aside every obstacle in order to reach Elisha and bring him to her child, so now we see her persistence in cutting through the royal red tape to get directly to the king with her request. It is not difficult to imagine her refusing to be deterred or delayed by the many servants and bureaucrats who cluttered the court; she proved her boldness once again by daring to interrupt the king's conversation with Gehazi.

In pursuing what she knew to be hers by right, her persistence paid off once again, for the king responded by instructing an official to "give back everything that belonged to her, including all the income from her land from the day she left the country until now" (2 Kings 8:6). This command suggests that it may have been the king himself who had possessed and profited from her land during her absence, as no other offender is named. In 1 Samuel 8:5 the Israelites demanded that Samuel appoint "a king to lead us such as all the other nations have," and God warned them that earthly kings would abuse them in various ways, including seizure of their best land (1 Sam. 8:14). In the case of the Shunammite, at least, we find a king who was willing to return the land with interest.

What readily persuaded this king to return the woman's land, aside from the obvious rightness of her cause and his own magnanimous spirit (or possibly his own guilty conscience)? Once again, we note God's marvelous providence in ordaining the "coincidence" by which the woman arrived to plead her case at the exact moment when Gehazi was recounting to the king the miracle of Elisha's restoration of her son some years before.

> The king was talking to Gehazi, the servant of the man of God, and had said, "Tell me about all the great things Elisha has done." Just as Gehazi was telling the king how Elisha had restored the dead to life, the woman whose son Elisha had brought back to life came to beg the king for her house and land. Gehazi said, "This is the woman, my lord the king, and this is

her son whom Elisha restored to life." The king asked
the woman about it, and she told him (2 Kings 8:4–6).

The perfect timing of the Shunammite's arrival both
confirmed Gehazi's story and assured the success of the
woman's mission. Our eternal, omnipresent God seems
to delight in ordering events within our finite time-and-
space framework to accomplish his will and bring glory
to his name. The Bible is filled with wonderful examples
such as this one that demonstrate his timely provision for
those who ask in faith for his help.

He provides for us in the same way today. It is as much
a miracle when we recognize God's unseen hand moving
within the natural world that he designed (see Rom. 8:28;
Rev. 4:11) as when he performs some extraordinary work
that seems to defy nature itself (e.g., when the sun stood
still for Joshua, Josh. 10:13; Moses' leprosy, Exod. 4:6–7;
and various restorations to life, 2 Kings 4, John 11:38–44).

The Shunammite's experiences demonstrate both types
of provision: first, God's miraculous restoration of life to
her dead son, through Elisha; and second, his perfect
timing of her appeal to coincide with Gehazi's account of
her story. Early in their friendship Elisha had offered to
speak to the king in her behalf when she actually needed
God's help (2 Kings 4:13). Now Elisha's influence was
effective as the woman spoke to the king about what God
had done. Her story blessed the king who in turn
blessed her with the return of her property.

How do we react to "coincidences"? What miracles is
God working in our lives right now? It is the Holy Spirit
who makes us aware of God's providence in ordinary as
well as extraordinary events, while we through grace

increase in knowledge and sensitivity. The Shunammite woman triumphed because of her preparation by faith and obedience, her persistence to know and attain God's will, and her increasing experience of God's power and provision. To receive the greatest blessing from this short, simple story, each of us would do well to evaluate the depth of her own faith. Let the Shunammite challenge us and stir us to action.

# 3

## Jochebed

### Primary Scripture Reading

Exodus 1, 2

### Supplementary References

Exodus 6
Exodus 7:7
Numbers 26:59
Hebrews 11:23

### Questions for Study and Discussion

**1.** Who were Jochebed and Amram? Describe the conditions facing the Hebrew nation in their day.

**2.** Why was the Egyptian pharaoh afraid? Were his fears justified, do you think? What did he do about his fears? Did his new policies improve the situation? Why or why not?

**3.** What children were already in Jochebed's family at the time of Moses' birth (see also Exod. 7:7)? Do you think Jochebed had to resort to extreme measures to save them, also?

**4.** Why did Jochebed defy the pharaoh's decree? Under what circumstances do you think you might disobey the civil law? Why?

**5.** List all the steps taken by Jochebed to save her baby. What other individuals helped her plan to succeed? What consequences could there have been if her plan had failed? What risks do you think you might take to rescue a person from physical or spiritual danger?

**6.** God's name is not mentioned in Jochebed's story. In what ways can you detect God's hand at work behind the scenes to preserve Moses' life? Is there a contradiction between a person's careful planning and having complete trust in God?

**7.** After he was rescued and restored to her, how, do you think, did Jochebed spend those early years with Moses before returning him to the palace? How did Moses later in his life demonstrate the influence of her early teaching? How are you using the time and influence you have with others to prepare them to know and do God's will?

The story of Jochebed gives us another perspective on faith: To believe that God is in perfect control of all things does *not* mean that we are merely automatons with no active role to play in his plan. Moses' mother was a shrewd, dynamic participant in the events related to her son's survival. Before we attempt to draw lessons from her example, we need to have a clear picture of the historical context and crisis of her story.

Exodus 1:5 records that seventy descendants of Jacob joined Joseph in Egypt and prospered there, becoming "exceedingly numerous" over several generations. At first, the entire family was welcomed cordially, because Joseph had been instrumental in helping Egypt plan wisely for the famine that so devastated other nations (read Gen. 37–50 for Joseph's fascinating life story). When Jacob and Joseph died, they were buried with highest royal ceremonies. But eventually a new ruler came to power who neither remembered the loyalty and wisdom of Joseph nor appreciated his numerous relatives. In fact, this pharaoh's three-pronged fear of the Israelites shows nothing less than paranoia: he feared that they would increase in number to the point of being uncontrollable by the Egyptians; he was afraid that in the event of a war the Israelites would join with the enemy against the Egyptians; and he feared that the Israelites would leave the country. Although unfounded, these fears led to the decision to oppress the Israelites and force them into subjection through bitter slavery (which eventually did lead to the realization of at least one of his fears, namely the departure from Egypt of the entire nation of Israel). Thus, the Hebrew slaves built the great store cities of Pithom and Rameses (Exod. 1:11) as well as other monuments to cruel labor. But the ruthlessness ("rigour", KJV) of the Egyptian slave drivers did not have the desired effect of decreasing the Hebrew population. Rather, the Israelites "multiplied and spread," increasing the Egyptians' "dread" (Exod. 1:12) all the more. The pharaoh then resorted to a second, more drastic strategy: selective infanticide. He ordered the Hebrew midwives, represented by Puah and Shiphrah, to kill all the boys born to the Israelites, but to allow the baby girls to live. Fortunately, these women proved they feared God more than the king, and disobeyed the command. For their daring faith they were rewarded with God's kindness to their own families and remembrance of their names in

Scripture. Pharaoh then turned to his own people to carry out his order to throw every Hebrew baby boy into the river (Exod. 1:22).

How long this ugly situation prevailed is not clear from the biblical record. In Exodus 2:1 we are introduced to a Levite man who married a Levite woman, presumably some time during this period of oppression. Their names, Amram and Jochebed, are not mentioned until Exodus 6:20 (which also makes note of the unusual fact that the bride was her husband's aunt—normally a relationship that was forbidden to marry, but not censured in this instance). Exodus 2:2 records that "she became pregnant and gave birth to a son." By crosschecking other verses, however, it becomes clear that this child is not Jochebed's firstborn, and not even her first son. A daughter Miriam is introduced as a child sufficiently mature to stand watch over Moses and then to propose to Pharaoh's daughter that Jochebed be hired as nursemaid for the baby. A very young child would have been incapable of handling such a crucial responsibility; Miriam was probably at least five years old or even older. Furthermore, Moses' brother Aaron was three years older than Moses (Exod. 7:7). So we are left to wonder whether the pharaoh's command was not yet in effect at the time of Aaron's birth, or to marvel at how Jochebed was able to save her firstborn son from death as well. We do have at least a glimpse into her character as we consider her careful and daring preparations for her second son. Once again we shall discover principles that will challenge our own lives.

Unlike several of the other women in this study, we do not find that Jochebed received any special direction from God concerning his purpose for Moses either before or after his birth. We might like to see her desperately clinging to God for comfort, or expressing her helplessness to face the Egyptian cruelties, with God providing new hope and a miraculous way of escape. Instead, we find a woman acting with quiet confidence to carry out her own plan to save her son. This does not mean that she either ignored or defied God's will, however. Even though there is no scene in the Bible record that depicts Jochebed communicating directly with the Lord, it is clear that she depended on his leading at every step. Her faith is portrayed not in her prayer life but in her practical life. The ten verses that express this quality in her character may be divided into three parts for our consideration.

## Deception

As soon as Moses was born, Jochebed "saw that he was a fine ('goodly', KJV) child" (Exod. 2:2). Hebrews 11:23 identifies a second factor at work in the parents' decision to conceal the baby: "By faith Moses' parents hid him for three months after he was born, because they saw he was no ordinary child and they were not afraid of the king's edict." Their faith, their trust in God, was greater than their fear of the Egyptian pharaoh.

Do you have such confidence in your Lord in the face of human opposition? Consider David's words:

What time I am afraid, I will trust in thee.
In God I will praise his word, in God I have put my trust;
 I will not fear what flesh can do unto me.

51

What time I am afraid, I will trust in thee.
In God I will praise his word, in God I have put my trust;
  I will not fear what flesh can do unto me.
In God I have put my trust:
  I will not be afraid what man can do unto me (Ps. 56:3,
  4, 11, KJV.)

Initially Jochebed's refusal to give up her baby was based primarily on love. Her strong maternal instinct would not allow her to part with him, even though at first she probably had no long-range plan to secure his safety. This new little life she had conceived and brought into the world was simply too precious to destroy. Even in our day, although the abortion rate is rising, many women who at first make the decision to destroy the life within them change their minds at the last instant. Mothers who consent to give up their babies for adoption often change their minds as well when they see the fruit of the creative miracle in which they have had a part. In spite of the great difficulties that they must face in raising the child, an overwhelming sense of protective love rises in response to God's "goodliness," and the bond is sealed forever.

Having committed herself permanently to preserving the life of her infant son, Jochebed probably did not have too much difficulty hiding him for the first few months, when a newborn can usually be kept fairly quiet with eating and sleeping around the clock. As he began to spend more time observing and exploring his world, however, his presence could not have been kept secret very long, especially with the whole Egyptian nation on the alert for Hebrew baby boys. To be discovered shelter-

ing Moses in defiance of the king's edict would undoubtedly have endangered the lives of Amram's entire family.
Even though they were not afraid, they were not safe. A
more permanent solution would have to be devised to
rescue Moses.

## Inception

As Moses' wakefulness increased, Jochebed's concern
must have increased also. Amram must have tried to
comfort both mother and son, but no way out of the crisis
was apparent until a bold idea occurred to Jochebed. If
Moses could somehow be placed under the personal
protection of Pharaoh himself, then surely he would be
exempt from the general death sentence! But how?
There was only one ray of hope—to attract the attention
of Pharaoh by appealing to the motherly instincts of his
own daughter, who might then plead the child's case
herself.

As the plan took shape, and the waterproof basket
was perfectly prepared to protect the baby, it was clear
that exact timing and placement were all-important.
Nothing could be left to chance. Undoubtedly, as much
prayer as care was devoted to the project. The daily habits of the royal princess would have to be carefully observed to determine her probable moods as well as her
routes. After a good meal, Moses was lulled to sleep and
placed in his little ark. Not cast adrift down the Nile to
feed a passing crocodile, he was nestled securely
"among the reeds along the bank" (Exod. 2:3). After
patient observation, Jochebed would have calculated the
most likely path Pharaoh's daughter would take to her

bath in the river, and placed Moses strategically in her way. Miriam was posted to wait and watch, carefully instructed in what and when to speak to the princess.

## Reception

The careful planning proved successful, as Pharaoh's daughter arrived at the river at exactly the right time and place to see the little basket. She sent her slave to fetch it out of the water and bring it to her. At the moment of discovery, Moses also played his part to perfection by starting to cry just as the princess opened the basket. "And behold, the babe wept. And she had compassion on him" (Exod. 2:6, KJV). Immediately he won her heart. There could be no doubt that he was a Hebrew, condemned to death by her own father. Nevertheless, the princess' original curiosity was transformed into tender pity toward his helplessness. When Miriam stepped out of her hiding place at this very moment of tenderness to propose finding a nursemaid for the baby, the princess yielded.

For the princess the baby may have meant only one more diversion, a human toy among a vast array of jewels and other entertainments; she may have cared nothing for the plight of the Israelites or the horror of her father's command. Whatever her motive, her act of restoration of the foundling to his mother's breast started ripples that culminated in tidal waves crashing on the seas of history for both Israel and Egypt. Similarly, individuals today may be as unaware of the far-reaching consequences that can develop from a single gesture of kindness offered at a key moment in God's eternal plan.

In this way Jochebed and Moses were quickly reunited, probably within minutes of his next scheduled meal, but this time with full palace approval. Jochebed was thus doubly recompensed for her careful efforts; not only was Moses' life spared, but Jochebed also received payment from the princess for nursing her own son.

Before weaning her son and returning him to the palace, Jochebed must have spent those precious early years teaching Moses about his people and his God, lessons that remained strong within him through eighty years of separation (first through forty years of Egyptian education and luxury, and then during the period of his isolation in Midian), until the Lord brought him back to lead his own people to freedom.

How careful are we to use the time we have with our little ones to equip them to serve God as he ordains? When he calls them to his service, are we then willing to turn them over to his care? Jochebed provides us a beautiful model and purpose for guiding our children at home while they are young. "Train a child in the way he should go: and when he is old, he will not turn from it" (Prov. 22:6). Some of us have more training time with our children than Jochebed had. Are we investing it with the same urgency to prepare them for the future ministry God has planned?

There are several other valuable lessons that may be drawn from a study of Jochebed. Moses' name itself brings out another theme of this story. The Hebrew root means *drawn out*, for as the princess said, "I drew him out of the water" (Exod. 2:10). One commentator has suggested that Moses was probably called by the syllable *ms* in the Egyptian language, meaning simply *child* or *son*

(*Unger's Bible Dictionary*, by Merrill F. Unger. Chicago: Moody, 1967, p. 759). He may also have received a much longer royal appellation during his life at court. In considering Exodus 2:9, however, it seems at least plausible that Pharaoh's daughter allowed Jochebed to suggest a suitable Hebrew name for the child. It would be consistent with Jochebed's method of careful planning for her to propose the very name by which she had called him from his birth, thus strengthening his Hebrew identity through his name as well as through his early training. Ironically, although Pharaoh had ordered all Hebrew baby boys to be thrown *into* the river, Jochebed had managed to have Pharaoh's daughter draw him *out* of it, to safety and ultimately to his destiny as God's chosen leader of the Hebrew nation in their going out of Egypt.

One other point must be stressed. God's name is not mentioned in any of the ten verses pertaining to Jochebed in the Bible. Yet his presence is all around her. It is he who showed kindness to the Hebrew midwives (Exod. 1:20), and he who heard the groaning of the Israelites because of the bitterness of their slavery (Exod. 2:24). But Jochebed seemed to stand and act independently throughout her portion of Exodus 2. How then can we call her a woman of faith? We know that our God is omnipresent and omnipotent, so we can be certain that it was his will, and not hers alone, that was accomplished in every detail of Jochebed's plan and its success. God's hand was needed to guide and direct *every* human actor in this moving drama.

Yet, to be an actor is not the same as to be a mere puppet. Jochebed was certainly not just a helpless bystander to Pharaoh's cruelty; neither was she only a means to achieve personal goals that were in tune with divine purposes. By means of her active faith she was privileged to cooperate with almighty God himself.

Similarly, we ought not to consider ourselves as merely anonymous, helpless, and hopeless blobs of humanity, but rather as coworkers with Christ for his glory, by his grace. "For we are God's fellow workers; you are God's field, God's building" (1 Cor. 3:9). "As God's fellow workers we urge you not to receive God's grace in vain" (2 Cor. 6:1). God has created each one of us with gifts and resources to accomplish great feats that attest to his power and love. Rather than obliterating our personalities, this truth calls us to our highest level of fulfillment, for we are free to choose to align ourselves with the one who has called us into being. Like Jochebed, we can dare to act on our faith, implementing his plans with the full exertion of our abilities, and joyfully claiming God's promise that he will "work in [us] to will and to act according to his good purpose" (Phil. 2:13).

Finally, Jochebed's selection of Pharaoh's own daughter as the means of salvation for Moses, when Pharaoh himself was the cruelest enemy of Israel, must have seemed bizarre, risky, or even crazy to her friends, if indeed Jochebed chose to confide her plan to them either before or after its inception. Will you take courage from her example, and dare to be creatively unusual and bold as you step out in faith to deal with the crises in your life, planning carefully and acting confidently, instead of wringing your hands in helpless despair? Do you pray and *give* up, resigned to your fate? Or do you pray and *get* up and get busy with the urgent tasks at hand? *You* are not strong enough to change yourself or your circumstances, but God *is*. Admitting your weakness, will you allow him to pour out his power through you to achieve his purposes?

When confronted with her very serious circumstances, Jochebed never projected the thought "It's hopeless. My son is doomed. There is nothing I can do about this." Instead, she seemed to reflect the same poised confidence Paul expressed in Philippians 4:13: "I can do *everything* through him who gives me strength." In your difficult situation today, let your response of daring, faith-filled action attract attention and accomplish God's design through a princess, overruling whatever obstacles a pharaoh may set in your path.

# PART TWO

# Women Rejected
# or Set Aside

Hagar

Zipporah

Job's Wife

Leah

In the title of this section the words *rejected* and *set aside* are in the passive voice. Someone other than the women themselves did the rejecting or setting aside. These women were acted upon; they were objects rather than subjects of activity. But were they truly innocent bystanders, mere victims of circumstances beyond their control?

We shall consider to what extent each of these four women contributed to her own difficulties. What was there about the attitudes and actions of Hagar, Zipporah, and Job's wife that made them unsuitable partners for God's service with Abraham, Moses, and Job? How does Leah demonstrate a better reaction to rejection than the other three women? What can we learn from these women that can help us in situations where we may feel ineffective, unappreciated, or somehow cut off from God's daily blessings?

# 4

## Hagar

### Primary Scripture Reading

Genesis 16:1–18; 18:15; 21

### Supplementary References

James 4:2–8
Isaiah 43:1–3
Hebrews 12:2, 3
1 Peter 5:6, 7

### Questions for Study and Discussion

**1.** What was Hagar's native land? What do you know about the range of duties and privileges she might have expected for herself in Abram's household?

**2.** What was she told to do for her master? Did she have any choice in the matter? Was this command out of the ordinary according to Hagar's culture and position? Did her status change as a result?

**3.** In which verse do you find a different attitude in Hagar than at first? Why did her feelings change? What happened as a direct result? Did Hagar have any control over these circumstances? Have you chosen to despise someone? What consequences ensued? If you feel you have suffered rejection, is there some action or an attitude on your part that contributed to that rejection? Could it have been avoided?

**4.** Compare God's two meetings with Hagar that are described in Genesis 16 and 21. What did he tell her to do? What was his purpose, do you think? Do you detect any spiritual development in Hagar in the second encounter as compared with the first?

**5.** Consider Ishmael's behavior and its consequences in Genesis 21:9. Whose attitude was he reflecting? In what ways have you noticed your feelings rubbing off on other people? Give some better ways of resolving your feelings.

**6.** What evidences of pride do you detect in Hagar's story? How is this sin connected with her rejection from Abraham's household? What significance do you find in the fact that Hagar found a wife in Egypt for Ishmael? Are there manifestations of pride in your life?

**7.** Compare the attitude expressed by Hagar's actions with the New Testament verses listed above, which present God's example and expectation of service. What lessons in humility do you need to apply to your life at home or at work today?

Being an Egyptian maidservant, Hagar had almost no part in the decisions concerning her household duties or personal life that her master and mistress, Abram and Sarai, made. In the culture of that time and place it was not unusual for a man to have sexual relations with any and all of the women in his household; multiple wives, concubines, or whole harems of slaves or captives are frequently mentioned in the Bible. This practice, though common, was never endorsed by God, however. Numerous passages indicate his high standard of monogamy (Gen. 2:24; Deut. 17:16–17; 1 Tim. 3:12).

The essential purpose of marriage, in the minds of Abram's contemporaries, was for a man to produce legitimate children, preferably male offspring, to inherit and defend his name and possessions after him. The selection of one slave girl over another to accomplish this purpose—in case of a wife's failure in this requirement— might have been made in recognition of her beauty or loyalty, but it would not have constituted a major or unreasonable deviation from accepted behavior. It was quite common for a barren wife to adopt her slave's children as her own, as Sarai proposed (later Rachel and Leah did the same; see Gen. 30). For Hagar to serve the function of preserving the family line of Abram could have been just one of a number of household duties she was expected to perform. It was only the fact that Sarai and Abram failed to grasp the full miracle of God's promise to them, and instead resorted to methods of their own, that made their conduct wrong. Hagar's sin was not in conceiving and bearing a child to Abram, but in her arrogant behavior that followed both acts. Perhaps she had no voice concerning what was done to her, but she *did* have a choice regarding her response. Hagar chose to despise, to keep distant, and to disseminate hostility to the next generation.

## Choice to Despise

In Genesis 15, God promised Abram offspring as numerous as the stars of the heavens. A son would come from his own body, and his descendants would inherit the land of Canaan.

> Now Sarai, Abram's wife, had borne him no children. But she had an Egyptian maidservant named Hagar; so she said to Abram, "The LORD has kept me from having children. Go, sleep with my maidservant; perhaps I can build a family through her." Abram agreed to what Sarai said. So after Abram had been living in Canaan ten years, Sarai his wife took her Egyptian maidservant Hagar and gave her to her husband to be his wife. He slept with Hagar, and she conceived (Gen. 16:1–4).

Throughout this entire transaction Hagar was viewed by Sarai and Abram merely as a tool to gain a specific objective, a child. After ten years of childlessness in Canaan, Sarai finally suggested a new approach, and Abram carried it out. Apparently the Lord was not consulted, and neither was Hagar.

We might be inclined to sympathize with Hagar's plight if this scene of sexual exploitation were all that we knew about her. She loses our respect at once, however, when we read of the marked change in her attitude recorded afterwards in Genesis 16:4: "When she knew she was pregnant, she began to despise her mistress." Although she had not engineered her circumstances at the outset, she *was* responsible for making the situation intolerable for the entire household by her sudden switch from apparent compliance to open arrogance.

We know, because the whole story has been recorded and retold for centuries, that God had intended from the beginning to bless Abram through Sarai's own child by his miraculous "quickening" (KJV) of their bodies, and that Ishmael, Hagar's son, was never meant to be the child of promise (see Gen. 17:18–22; 21:12; also Gal. 4:22–31). Their alternate plan to use Hagar was indicative of their own undeveloped faith up to that time.

Nevertheless, Hagar had an active role in choosing to despise her mistress, and thereby bringing on herself an increase in suffering. Had she sought to overcome her emotions, she would probably not have incurred Sarai's "hardness" (KJV), which caused her first to flee to the wilderness (Gen. 16:5–6) and later to be sent forth with Ishmael (Gen. 21:9–14). Is there a person whom you have chosen to despise because of the way he or she has treated you? In what ways has your response made the situation better or worse for yourself and for others?

### Choice to Keep Distant

Once we realize that Hagar was her own catalyst, making her difficult situation worse, we can move on to consider whether she learned anything from the experiences of God meeting her twice in the wilderness. Two distinct passages record Hagar's encounters with God, which may be placed in a chart for comparison.

|  | Genesis 16:6–16 | Genesis 21:14–22 |
|---|---|---|
| *Why Hagar left:* | Sarai mistreated her. | Abraham sent her out with Ishmael, bread, and water. |
| *Where she went:* | Near a spring in the desert, beside the road to Shur | In the desert of Beersheba |

| How she felt: | Probable fear, self-pity | Expected the death of Ishmael, wept |
|---|---|---|
| What the angel of the LORD said: | "Hagar, servant of Sarai, where have you come from, and where are you going?"<br><br>"Go back to your mistress and submit to her. I will so increase your descendants that they will be too numerous to count. You are now with child and you will have a son. You shall name him Ishmael, for the LORD has heard of your misery. He will be a wild donkey of a man; his hand will be against everyone and everyone's hand against him, and he will live in hostility toward all his brothers." | "What is the matter, Hagar? Do not be afraid; God has heard the boy crying as he lies there. Lift the boy up and take him by the hand, for I will make him into a great nation." |
| What God did: | | Opened Hagar's eyes and she saw a well of water.<br>God was with the boy as he grew up. |
| Outcome: | Hagar gave a name to the LORD and to the well *Lahai Roi*, "the Living One who sees me." | Hagar got water for Ishmael. He grew up, lived in the desert and became an archer. While he was living in the Desert of Paran, his mother got a wife for him from Egypt. |

There is a lot we don't know about Hagar before, between, and after these encounters with the angel of the Lord. We cannot really judge her overall level of spiritual commitment. But in looking at the chart above, there does not seem to be any marked development in her relationship with God from the first of these experiences to the second, a separation of approximately fifteen years.

True, Hagar had not been called to a personal ministry by God. Being a foreigner, she should be given credit, at the least, for recognizing God's presence and following his direct commands—first to return to Sarai and name the child Ishmael, and later to get up and get water for her son. She responded honestly enough to God's inquiries and commands. But she did not grow to any deeper understanding of his person or plans, as Abraham and Sarah did. The last we are told of Hagar is that she provided Ishmael with a wife from Egypt, her own place of origin. We would have expected the same had she never interacted at all with her master and mistress or their God.

Are you content to have a static relationship with God from year to year? In what ways has your awareness of his love deepened in the last five, fifteen or even thirty years, so that you depend more joyfully, and less nervously, on his concern and care? Do you worship him, but expect him to keep his distance and not interfere with your self-determined personality and plans, and not instruct you to deal with the difficult people and circumstances in your life?

Hagar's experiences help me to realize that not only does God want to meet me wherever I am, but also that he wants me to yield and grow closer to him as he leads me each step and each year of my life. He will not force his will on me, just as he did not compel Hagar. But the choice is mine to open the door to receive him when he knocks (see Rev. 3:20).

God was knocking at the door of Hagar's heart when the angel spoke to her on those two occasions we have studied, but she never really admitted him into her life. How can we know this? Although she surely thought and said more than is attributed to her in the biblical narrative, it is interesting to look for an answer in the comments that are included. She is quoted twice in Genesis 16. In verse 8 she responded to God's question with the words, "I'm running away from my mistress Sarai." In verse 13 she gave God a special name and said, "I have now seen the One who sees me." And just before the angel met with her again in Genesis 21, Hagar thought to herself, "I cannot watch the boy die" (Gen. 21:16).

Each of these statements begins with the subject *I*, referring to Hagar. They are simple declarative statements of fact. Hagar never seemed to express her own needs or to ask for God's help in any way, even though her anguish must have been profound on both occasions. Why did she not call on the Lord to provide comfort and care for herself and her son?

We would do well to ask ourselves the same question when we experience periods of either simple discouragement or real rejection. There is no doubt that God's resources to help us are boundless; yet he always desires that we first come to him acknowledging our utter helplessness and humbly seeking his forgiveness, comfort, guidance, strength, and provision (Matt. 11:28–30; James 4:8). Then he is pleased to fill our cups to overflowing (Ps. 23), to do whatever we ask in his name. James confirmed this sequence when he observed, "You do not have because you do not ask God" (James 4:2). Instead of asking and receiving, Hagar chose to keep her distance.

## Choice to Disseminate Hostility

We have seen that Hagar chose to despise her mistress and to keep aloof from the personal, powerful God who had twice revealed himself to her. Both choices have important lessons for us today. What else can we learn from this rejected woman?

On the feast day that celebrated Isaac's weaning, Sarah observed Hagar's son "mocking" (Gen. 21:9). Although not all translations of the Bible agree on this word, it is clear that Ishmael did something to rekindle the antagonism that apparently had been smoldering beneath the surface for many years. Whatever it was that he did, his behavior so offended Sarah that she insisted Abraham send him and his mother away once and for all. "Get rid of that slave woman and her son, for that slave woman's son will never share in the inheritance with my son Isaac" (Gen. 21:10).

It would be difficult to imagine any other source of Ishmael's attitude of superiority than his own mother. Although she had managed not to anger Sarah overtly during those intervening years (at least, no further confrontations are recorded in Scripture), it appears that Hagar could not resist sharing her private opinions with Ishmael, who readily adopted her attitudes. She had submitted outwardly, but not inwardly, and thus had transmitted her inner poison to her son.

This pattern reminds me of the story of a small boy whose father attempted to punish him by making him sit in a corner. The boy defiantly insisted on standing, and his father repeatedly shoved him into the chair. After several rounds, the child finally remained in his seat, but was heard to mutter, "I'm sitting on the outside, Pa, but inside I'm still standing."

Here we find another challenge for our lives as we consider Hagar's example. In what ways are you still "standing on the inside" against the authority of God, so that your bad moods and negative attitudes are never healed but continue to fester and poison your life and the lives of others? Instead, will you now choose to pour out your feelings of hurt and rejection to God, who not only sees you but knows your very heart? He can soothe and heal only if you allow him to work his will in your spirit as well as in your difficult situation. Yield yourself fully to him, and claim the full measure of comfort offered in Isaiah 43:1–3:

> Fear not, for I have redeemed you; I have called you by name; you are mine. When you pass through the waters, I will be with you; and when you pass through the rivers, they will not sweep over you. When you walk through the fire, you will not be burned; the flames will not set you ablaze. For I am the LORD, your God, the Holy One of Israel, your Savior.

One last thought. Hagar was a servant, yet she did not have a servant's heart. Christ, in washing the disciples' feet, showed them and us his new standard of humility and service (John 13:1–17). When we feel rejected or depressed, and most of us do from time to time, what a privilege it is to contemplate his perfect example of suffering and submission on our behalf.

> Let us fix our eyes on Jesus, the author and perfecter of our faith, who for the joy set before him endured the cross, scorning its shame, and sat down at the right hand of the throne of God. Consider him who endured such opposition from sinful men, so that you will not grow weary and lose heart (Heb. 12:2–3).

Our suffering, whether due to our own sin or to circumstances over which we have no control, pales in comparison with what Christ endured for us. No matter how many years we must wait in hardship, we can be confident of his continued presence with us, and our eternal presence with him. "Humble yourselves, therefore, under God's mighty hand, that he may lift you up in due time. Cast all your anxiety on him because he cares for you" (1 Peter 5:6–7).

# 5

## Zipporah

### Primary Scripture Reading

Exodus 3, 4, and 18

### Supplementary Reference

2 Corinthians 6:14

### Questions for Study and Discussion

**1.** Who was Zipporah? Whom did she marry? Why? Do you think she was well suited to be the wife of such a man? Why or why not?

**2.** Read the passage about the circumcision of Moses' son (Exod. 4) in as many different translations as you can. Why was it necessary? What attitude do you think lay behind Zipporah's words and actions in that scene? Was she being obedient or defiant? Of whom?

**3.** Why didn't Zipporah participate in the exodus from Egypt with Moses? Did someone send her back to Midian, or did she refuse to go on with her husband?

**4.** Think about some of your personal and professional relationships. How could you convince your partner to carry out

God's will without your destroying the partnership? What warnings do you draw from Zipporah's example concerning God's standard of "equal yoking" (see 2 Cor. 6:14)?

**5.** Perhaps Zipporah's behavior could be explained in terms of her lack of trust in Moses or in God. Was it fair for her to be excluded from the exodus for this reason, rather than to be given the opportunity to develop her faith? What do you learn about God's requirement of faith from this story? Are you going forward or backward in your spiritual life?

**6.** How do you interpret the reunion of Moses with his wife, children, and father-in-law after the exodus (Exod. 18)? Did any members of Zipporah's family stay with Moses during the years of wandering in the desert? Why, or why not?

Zipporah is mentioned in three separate chapters of Exodus. Moses married her, returned to Egypt without her, and had a brief reunion with her after he successfully led the Israelites to freedom. The adage "Behind every great man is a great woman" can be applied literally to Zipporah—Moses left her *far* behind! How did she miss out on becoming a full partner in her husband's great mission, and what can we learn from her example?

### Family Background

First, we need to consider Moses himself. When he was forty years old he killed an Egyptian guard who was beating a Hebrew slave, and fled the country. It was his choice to marry Zipporah and work as a shepherd for her father Jethro (or Reuel) for forty years before God called him back to Egypt (see Acts 7:29–34 as well as

Exod. 1–3 for the context). But Moses' idea was not to abandon his wife in Midian just so he could go after fame and fortune in his homeland. In fact, God had quite a hard time convincing Moses to go, and had to promise him three signs in addition to the oratorical support of his brother Aaron before he agreed. Even so, Moses begged, "O Lord, please send someone else to do it" (Exod. 4:13).

Moses' humility was reflected throughout his period of leadership. He was acutely aware of his own verbal deficiencies. "O LORD, I have never been eloquent, neither in the past nor since you have spoken to your servant. I am slow of speech and tongue" (Exod. 4:10). He depended on Aaron's help in speaking to the Egyptian rulers as well as to his own people. His sister Miriam also shared some of the responsibilities of leadership with him. In addition, he welcomed a suggestion from his father-in-law to appoint captains and judges to lighten his burden. Numbers 12:3 states, "Now Moses was a very humble man, more humble than anyone else on the face of the earth." All this evidence demonstrates the fact that Moses needed and appreciated the support of his family. God's summons to Moses to return to Egypt in no way provided him with an ego trip or a deliberate attempt to reject the wife and lifestyle he had enjoyed in Midian. Moses would not have chosen to set aside Zipporah had she not shown herself to be ineligible to join with him in fulfilling God's appointed task.

What do we actually know about Zipporah? Technically, she was not an Israelite, nor did she experience bondage with them in Egypt. Her father was Jethro, a priest of the Midianites, who were descended from the fourth son of Abraham by Keturah (q.v.). The Midianites were closely connected with the Ishmaelites in Arabia (see Gen. 37). Because of this association we might say that strong regional, if not racial or religious ties, prevailed to keep Zipporah at home, or possibly prevented her from generating much sympathy for the plight of the Israelites in Egypt. We could then point to her example as evidence of the incompatibility that is bound to emerge in a marriage of a believer with an unbeliever (see 2 Cor. 6:14).

Family background is really too simplistic an explanation of Zipporah's disqualification, however. With the same history, both her father and her brother became much more enthusiastically and extensively involved with Moses and the Israelites. After the exodus, Jethro's reunion with his son-in-law was ebullient.

> Now Jethro, the priest of Midian and father-in-law of Moses, heard of everything God had done for Moses and for his people Israel, and how the LORD had brought Israel out of Egypt. . . . Jethro was delighted to hear about all the good things the LORD had done for Israel in rescuing them from the hand of the Egyptians. He said, "Praise be to the LORD, who rescued you from the hand of the Egyptians and of Pharaoh, and who rescued the people from the hand of the Egyptians. Now I know that the LORD is greater than all other gods, for he did this to those who had treated Israel arrogantly" (Exod. 18:1, 9–11).

They sacrificed and ate together in the presence of God with all the elders of Israel.

In the midst of this scene of celebration, Zipporah is mentioned only in passing, and somewhat cooly.

> After Moses had sent away his wife Zipporah, his father-in-law Jethro received her and her two sons. . . . Jethro, Moses' father-in-law, together with Moses' sons and wife, came to him in the desert where he was camped near the mountain of God. Jethro had sent word to him, "I, your father-in-law Jethro, am coming to you with your wife and her two sons." So Moses went out to meet his father-in-law and bowed down and kissed him. . . . Moses told his father-in-law about everything the LORD had done to Pharaoh and the Egyptians for Israel's sake and about all the hardships they had met along the way and how the LORD had saved them (Exod. 18:2–8).

It seems that Zipporah was present but not a full participant in the welcoming party. The father-in-law's relationship with Moses was both warmer and deeper.

Similarly, Jethro's son Hobab (presumably Zipporah's brother and therefore Moses' brother-in-law) apparently continued his association with the Israelites for an even longer period. In Numbers 10:29–33, Moses begged him to remain as their guide, promising to share with him "whatever good things the LORD gives us." Although Hobab's initial response was, "No, I will not go. I am going back to my own land and my own people" (Num. 10:30), he apparently traveled with them for some time. Later, Hobab's descendants, the Kenites, are remembered for their kindness to Israel (Judg. 4:9–24 and 1 Sam. 15:6). Family ties cannot be blamed for Zipporah's detachment from her husband's assigned purpose.

## Holding Back

Ethnic identity is never God's primary criterion for inclusion among his chosen people; rather, personal faith was and is the sole standard. Zipporah did not share with Moses the personal faith in God necessary to support his unique ministry or even to survive the arduous journey and trials which lay ahead for him.

Jesus warned, "No man can serve two masters. Either he will hate the one and love the other, or he will be devoted to the one and despise the other" (Matt. 6:24). He offers us a choice between God and Mammon. In Moses' case, Zipporah was functioning in the role of Mammon, the pull of the world and its desires. Moses (or any husband) could not sustain for long the tension between the leading forward of God and the pulling back of his wife. It seems that she was not able to release her husband *wholeheartedly* to the Lord, a problem that is both familiar and challenging for us today. Moses had to make the difficult decision to send her back to Jethro in order to fulfill God's greater purpose for his own life and for his people.

How can I infer that Zipporah would have interfered with Moses' ministry? Because she did so, in an important incident recorded in a confusing passage in Exodus 4. Let us consider several translations of verses 24–26, in order better to understand the event and its implications.

And it came to pass by the way in the inn, that the LORD met him [Moses] and sought to kill him. Then Zipporah took a sharp stone, and cut off the foreskin of her son, and cast it at his feet, and said, Surely a bloody husband . . . thou art, because of the circumcision (King James Version).

At a lodging place on the way the LORD met him and sought to kill him. Then Zipporah took a flint and cut off her son's foreskin, and touched Moses' feet with it and said, "Surely you are a bridegroom of blood," . . . because of the circumcision (Revised Standard Version).

At an inn on the way the LORD met him and was at the point of taking his life; but Zipporah took a flint knife, circumcised her son and threw the foreskin at his feet with the words, "You are indeed a blood bridegroom to me." Then he let him alone when she said, because of the circumcision, "You are my bridegroom in blood" (Modern Language).

As Moses and his family were traveling along and had stopped for the night, Jehovah appeared to Moses and threatened to kill him. Then Zipporah his wife took a flint knife and cut off the foreskin of her young son's penis, and threw it against Moses' feet, remarking, disgustedly, "What a blood-smeared husband you've turned out to be!" Then God let him alone (Living Bible).

At a lodging place on the way, the LORD met Moses and was about to kill him. But Zipporah took a flint knife, cut off her son's foreskin and touched Moses' feet with it. "Surely you are a bridegroom of blood to me," she said. So the LORD let him alone. (At that time she said "bridegroom of blood," referring to circumcision) (New International Version).

The problem here is not to choose our favorite version but the most accurate. Rather than becoming more confused, I hope we can have greater respect and appreciation for the difficult task of Bible translation through this exercise. This passage is important to our understanding of Moses, Zipporah, and God himself.

Several questions may be raised. Why would God call Moses to return to Egypt and then try to kill him on the way? How did Zipporah know that circumcising their son Gershom would gain Moses' release from the Lord? Was she right in performing the rite? What attitudes toward Moses and toward God were reflected in her actions? The various texts offer us several possible interpretations with only partial information. Still, several observations can be made about this incident that may provide useful applications to various situations in our lives.

Everything I know about God's character tells me that he was not trying to kill Moses, but only wanted to get his attention about a serious matter that needed to be dealt with before he got all the way to Egypt. God had commanded circumcision of all Hebrew males as a sign of his covenant with Abraham (see Gen. 17:9–14). It was to be performed on the eighth day of life, or upon conversion. Moses had failed to obey this commandment in regard to his sons prior to his trip, but it was an act that was essential not only for his own training but also for the Egyptians' understanding of the importance of the covenant, and for the credibility of Moses as a leader in the eyes of the Israelites.

Zipporah seems to have saved Moses' life by performing the circumcision of Gershom just in time. Why was she not appreciated for her quick-thinking rescue? For one thing, circumcision was a male-only activity. Women were excluded from participation at every level—as patient, witness, or surgeon. But it was her attitude rather than her act that caused Zipporah to be sent back to Jethro with her sons. There was a touch of bitterness and reproach as she threw the bloody foreskin at Moses' feet with an air of "Now look what I had to do to save your neck!" Again we see a wife who obeyed God in her deed but not in her heart, which was, and is, not enough for the Lord.

Zipporah had started out on the journey to Egypt with Moses. After the incident at the inn she turned around and went back to her father's house. Exodus 18:2 informs us, "After Moses had sent away his wife Zipporah, his father-in-law Jethro received her and her two sons." It is not clear from the passage in Exodus 4 whether God sent her home, whether Moses refused to let her continue with him, or whether she herself changed her mind about the journey. There is no indication that Zipporah objected to the decision or pleaded for another chance to remain at his side.

The crisis must have revealed to each of them the personal cost of obedience to God. Moses chose to obey. Zipporah did not take that step of faith with him, even though she had acted quickly to save his life. Her outburst expressed her strong, if subconscious, desire not to follow where God and her husband were leading. Perhaps she was even thinking to herself, "For richer, for poorer, but not for this!" as she drew the line that cut off their relationship.

Try to evaluate honestly before God your relationship with the members of your family. Are there limits to how far *you* are willing to go to help your spouse, children, or friends respond to God's direction? Do you offer your wholehearted support, or do you sometimes pull against their commitment to serve God first—an effort to keep at least a corner of the attention on yourself? Is your own commitment wholeheartedly focussed on God, or are you too easily distracted by the impression you are trying to make on others? Be careful that you do not put your loved ones in the position of having to choose between satisfying you and serving God.

Zipporah failed to go to Egypt with her husband, but she did have another opportunity to join him after his return, as we have seen in Exodus 18:5–6. It is difficult to determine whether she went back to Midian with Jethro or continued through the wilderness with the Israelites. The Bible does not mention her again. Exodus 18:27 states, "Then Moses sent his father-in-law on his way, and he returned to his own country," without specifying whether Zipporah stayed with her husband or went with her father. My guess is that she parted from Moses a second time. Had she remained, more should have been recorded of her, including some record of her death, if not other incidents. In particular, it would seem that the story of the confrontation of Aaron and Miriam over Moses' Cushite wife (Num. 12:1) would have contained some mention of Zipporah had she still been part of the family at that point. Throughout the account of her life Moses just doesn't seem to pay her much attention either at the time of their reunion or afterwards.

Zipporah's rejection, both *of* and *by* Moses, was largely of her own making. Even though I wish that the account were more complete so that I could know for certain what became of her, I do not suppose, from reading the passages we do have, that Zipporah was any more capable of joining her husband on the journey to the Promised Land than of traveling to Egypt to take part in the exodus. Lacking a personal relationship of total trust with God, she was not able to look or move toward a new horizon in either direction. Thus, she was set aside from service. Where is God trying to move you? Are you willing to go, or will you be left behind or left out when others step forward in obedience?

# 6

## Job's Wife

### Primary Scripture Reading

Job 1, 2, and 42

### Supplementary Reference

Matthew 16:23

### Questions for Study and Discussion

**1.** Describe Job's family and property, using the first five verses of Job 1. List some of his blessings. What did he do regularly in behalf of his children? What did this practice show about Job's relationship with God?

**2.** What arrangement did the Lord make with Satan concerning Job? Did Job deserve to be treated this way? Why did God allow this test of his servant? What limitation did God place on Satan's power to afflict Job?

**3.** List the sequence of catastrophes that befell Job, using Job 1:13–2:8. Why, do you think, was Job's wife not struck down with the rest of the family? Was it in Satan's interest to let her live?

**4.** What was the advice Job's wife gave to her husband in 2:9? Can you explain his response to her and the comment he made in 2:10? How are these verses similar to Christ's words to Peter in Matthew 16:23? What is the source of the advice you offer to your friends and family members?

**5.** If you have time, skim through the arguments of Job's friends, Job's defense, and God's confrontation of Job in chapters 3–41. What does Job learn from his sufferings?

**6.** What happened to Job at the end of the book (Job 42:10–17)? Is the mother of his new family the same woman as the wife mentioned in chapter 2? Why, or why not, do you think?

**7.** Did Job's wife benefit in any way from her experiences? In what ways, do you think, did she help or hinder her husband in his sufferings? What do you learn about God from the example of her life? How can you be sure to give godly advice that others will follow?

The Book of Job is a literary masterpiece of suffering and searching, as well as a philosophical penetration into the nature of God and his dealings with humanity. It has much to teach us that would merit a deeper study than we can attempt in this chapter. Our purpose is to focus on the character of Job's wife, and to apply the warning of her example to our own lives.

There are two important questions to consider. First, why was Job's wife spared, when all the rest of Job's family, crops, servants, flocks, and physical health were destroyed by Satan? Second, although Job's wife was not physically cast out, she was sternly rebuked for the poor advice she offered her husband; therefore, what wrong attitudes were revealed in her single comment that made Job react strongly and that resulted in her being left out of the rest of the narrative? Although she did not die and was not divorced, she does not appear in the story again.

Even though we infer that she is the same wife who provided Job with ten children at the end of the book, she is not mentioned as a full partner in his blessing from God.

As we look for answers to these challenging questions we must be mindful of the fact that only two verses concern Job's wife in the entire book; and we must be on our guard against irresponsible interpretation or distortion of the context. Whatever we suppose must have happened should always be laid before God, so that we remain open to receive whatever he would teach us through this woman.

## Spared by Satan

Satan's challenge to God was that he could compel Job to curse God to his face if only Satan were given permission to touch (i.e., destroy) Job's assets—his personal family, wealth, and health. God showed his confidence in Job through his willingness to allow such a test. The single restriction on the test was that Job's life might not be taken.

Immediately Job received back-to-back messages that all of his flocks, crops, servants, and children had been destroyed (Job 1:13–19). His response to this devastating news is amazing.

> At this, Job got up and tore his robe and shaved his head. Then he fell to the ground in worship and said: "Naked I came from my mother's womb, and naked I will depart. The LORD gave and the LORD has taken away; may the name of the LORD be praised." In all

this, Job did not sin by charging God with wrongdoing (Job 1:20–22).

In order to win his wager, Satan clearly needed to try another strategy, and for this purpose he had craftily preserved an "ace-in-the-hole"—Job's wife. Nothing in his bargain with God would have prevented him from killing her along with Job's ten children; only because of the possibility of his accomplishing more evil by using her to influence her husband to curse God did Satan spare her life. Since the initial, external assault on Job had failed to achieve the desired effect, Satan turned his efforts in a new direction: destroying Job's integrity.

We don't see Satan appearing in physical form to tempt Job's wife as he did with Eve. But consider how well she served his purposes. Her statement "Curse God and die!" (Job 2:9) is the only instance recorded in the book in which Satan's objective was explicitly articulated to Job. If instead of simply scanning the list of his afflictions we can appreciate the depth of his agony, we will have some idea of the strength of the temptation to follow his wife's advice. Had Job yielded at that point Satan would have been the victor, and the whole book, indeed the whole world, would have proceeded very differently. We can thank God for protecting us from such horrible speculations.

But the fact that Satan could even attempt to ruin a man's relationship with God by exploiting his relationship of trust with his wife is a strong challenge to me to share only God's wisdom with my family and friends, and to beware of false influences. If Satan spared Job's wife because he thought he could work greater harm through her than without her, I must be watchful for what evil he may be trying to accomplish through me. Watchful, but not fearful, however, since I can be confident that Christ has already won the final victory over sin and death (Heb. 2:14–15).

## Spurned by Spouse

Apart from serving Satan's purpose in his wager with God, what was there about his wife's advice that caused such a strong rejection from Job? In a word, blasphemy. God had clearly set forth the punishment for such a crime against his name.

> If anyone curses his God, he will be held responsible: anyone who blasphemes the name of the LORD must be put to death. The entire assembly must stone him. Whether an alien or native-born, when he blasphemes the Name, he must be put to death (Lev. 24:15–16).

Many other verses in the Bible elaborate on God's severe view of blasphemy, including Exodus 20:1–7 (part of the Ten Commandments) and Matthew 12:30–32, where Jesus said:

> "He who is not with me is against me, and he who does not gather with me scatters. And so I tell you, every sin and blasphemy will be forgiven men, but the blasphemy against the Spirit will not be forgiven. Anyone who speaks a word against the Son of Man will be forgiven, but anyone who speaks against the Holy Spirit will not be forgiven, either in this age or in the age to come."

There can be no mercy for one who curses the name of our maker and model for holiness. Yet this is what Job's wife precisely and deliberately suggested that he do—"Curse God and die!" Fortunately, Job rejected her advice with all the strength of his being. "'You are talking like a foolish woman. Shall we accept good from God, and not trouble?' In all this, Job did not sin in what he said" (Job 2:10).

## Stuck in Suffering

How could a wife respond to her husband's suffering in such an unsympathetic way? Her comment was actually a reflection of her own despair. Since Job must have shared all of his children, servants, and flocks with his wife, she, too, had lost everything. Yet, we do not see her progressing out of her profound grief and confusion to a place of acceptance and worship, as Job did throughout the course of the book. Her outburst in favor of blasphemy suggests that she turned instead in the direction of hopeless bitterness. She saw no possibility of discovering any explanations for her troubles, and she had no faith to believe that God *was* in control, even though his purposes and plans were beyond her comprehension. Without any way to deal with their mutual suffering, she was unable to cope with the additional agony of Job's painful sores (Job 2:7). One more undeserved disaster, one more unanswered question were more than she could bear. Unwilling to expose her wounds before the Lord in order to receive his comfort, she could never comprehend, not to mention share, Job's attitude of long-suffering and faith. From such a state it is but a small step downward to the conclusion that nothing has meaning, and then just another step to open disobedience or defiance of God (with the argument "If nothing matters, what is the point of obedience?"). To Job's wife, an early death, even by stoning or the striking of God's hand against her husband, seemed preferable to his unrelenting agony.

Be honest. Have you ever felt this way? Disease, disaster, and despair threaten to swallow you up, until death itself seems to offer the only way of escape. Listen to God. For the hurt there is hope, for the fear faith. He does not promise a walk down Easy Street the moment you put your hand in his. It may be down Hard Road instead, but he is always with you. Though your grasp may falter at times, his hold on you is everlasting.

> Yea, though I walk through the valley of the shadow of death, I will fear no evil: for thou art with me; thy rod and thy staff they comfort me. Thou preparest a table before me in the presence of mine enemies: thou anointest my head with oil; my cup runneth over. Surely goodness and mercy shall follow me all the days of my life: and I will dwell in the house of the LORD for ever (Ps. 23:4–6, KJV).

## Shortsighted Suggestion

In addition to being stuck in her own suffering, Job's wife seemed determined to impress on Job the hopelessness of his situation. Without being able to see out of her own hole, she discouraged him from looking beyond his misery. Entrenched in her own grief, she offered no sympathy, no comfort, no sensitivity whatsoever to her husband's needs. She had to be sure that Job was well aware of her negative outlook, but she was not open to being comforted or guided by her husband's larger view or by God's perfect perspective.

Often I find myself acting too much like a mother hen clucking over her chicks. I offer profound insights into other peoples' lives free for the taking (and they are worth the fee!). Always on the alert to insure that my children, husband, and friends behave and learn appropriately from every situation, I may miss an important lesson for my own life. Job's wife thought she knew what Job ought to do, but she was quite blind to her own need. She reminds me that my first responsibility is to be more open to what the Lord would teach *me,* and more relaxed in allowing him to guide his other children directly and according to his own perfect will for them.

Job's wife had blocked herself off from the Lord's comfort and was trying to interfere in his relationship with Job as well. For his part, Job was in a state of shock, confusion, and pain: yet, he was willing to let God enlighten him through his experiences (see Prov. 2:1–8). He answered his wife appropriately. "You are talking like a foolish woman. Shall we accept good from God, and not trouble?" (Job 2:10). A footnote in the New International Version points out that his word *foolish* actually denotes *moral deficiency,* an apt description of her character.

If Satan spared Job's wife because of his mischief, God spared her because of his mercy. As far as her advice and her personality are concerned, she became of no account at that very point in the narrative. She is referred to later, however (in Job 19:17 and 31:10), and she must have survived to bear Job's subsequent children of blessing (Job 42:12–13). Still, her wrong attitude caused her to lose all opportunity for development, both as an individual and as a character in the book.

Job's friends were more persistent with their false accusations and poor advice than was Job's wife. They were sternly rebuked by God for their wrong judgments. "I am angry with you . . . because you have not spoken of me what is right, as my servant Job has" (Job 42:7). They were wrong, but they became reconciled at the end when God accepted Job's sacrifice and intercessory prayer in their behalf and allowed them to celebrate his double portion of prosperity. From their story we should learn not that it is wrong to question God but that it is wrong to refuse to heed his answers.

To speak the truth about God requires diligent study and prayer. It is not easy to keep from embroidering his Word with our own thoughts and desires or from wallowing in our own experiences. But the tremendous challenge of Job's wife is that if we fail to fulfill the important responsibility of leading others to praise rather than to curse God's name, Satan is only too happy to add more aces to his deck of destruction. On the other hand, God desires

to comfort all who mourn,
  and provide for those who grieve in Zion—
to bestow on them a crown of beauty instead of ashes,
  the oil of gladness instead of mourning,
  and a garment of praise instead of a spirit of despair.
They will be called oaks of righteousness, a planting
  of the LORD for the display of his splendor (Isa. 61:2–3).

93

Will you allow him to do this in your life, so that you do not find yourself set aside in the same way as Job's wife, and for the same reason?

# 7

## Leah

### Primary Scripture Reading

Genesis 29–44

### Supplementary Reference

Philippians 4

### Questions for Study and Discussion

**1.** Skim Genesis 29 and 30, noting verses that give details about the appearance and character of the sister-wives Rachel and Leah. Which woman do you think you most closely resemble? Which woman provides the more godly example?

**2.** Describe their father Laban, using these chapters and anything else you remember about him. Why did he deceive Jacob in this way?

**3.** How, do you think, did Leah initially feel about her father's trick and Jacob's reaction? Did anything happen in the course of time to change her predicament? Could she have done anything to improve her situation?

**4.** What was the constant desire of Leah's heart? Do you think she ever achieved her goal? Did the effects of Jacob's favoritism diminish after Rachel's death?

**5.** What does the scene concerning the mandrakes signify to you (Gen. 30:14–16)? What insights into the personalities of the two women and the social dynamics of Jacob's household do you get from this passage?

**6.** If your Bible translation has footnotes or marginal references, trace the meanings of the names Leah gave to her children and those of her handmaid. What evidence of Leah's manner of coping with her feelings of rejection do you find? How did God comfort her? Through which of her offspring did God choose to send the Messiah (Gen. 49:10–12; Mic. 3:2; Rev. 5:5)? How would that fact have been an extra blessing to Leah had she known it?

**7.** Have you, like Leah, been rejected in some way? How could you apply her example, and experience God's comfort, in the midst of your difficult circumstances?

Genesis 29 tells how Jacob met and fell in love with his cousin and endured seven years of hard labor to win her as his bride. His deep love and devotion to Rachel have inspired marriage dreams and promises ever since that day. Then there was Leah. Her story can also inspire us by showing us the way to turn over to God our feelings of hurt and rejection.

We have seen in our study so far that Hagar, Zipporah, and Job's wife had to be sent away, sent back, or totally ignored because their personalities or advice were incompatible with God's purposes. They could not ultimately contradict his plans, but neither did they cooperate fully with them. Leah's situation was different. She was willing to obey her father, her husband, and her God, but she experienced rejection anyway, in that her husband Jacob always preferred her sister. This prejudice was undeserved, but no less painful. The way Leah learned to deal with her unhappiness through many years can encourage each one of us whenever we feel unjustly unappreciated.

## Face Facts

Laban, Rebekah's brother and the father of Rachel and Leah, is a complex character worthy of study in his own right. For our purposes, however, it is sufficient to note from the passages in which he is mentioned (Gen. 24–31, passim) that he was wealthy, powerful, and used to getting his own way, which was usually devious. Consider the record of Jacob's initial interviews with his father-in-law.

As soon as Laban heard the news about Jacob, his sister's son, he hurried to meet him. He embraced him and kissed him and brought him to his home, and there Jacob told him all these things. Then Laban said to him, "You are my own flesh and blood." After Jacob had stayed with him for a whole month, Laban said to him, "Just because you are a relative of mine, should you work for me for nothing? Tell me what your wages should be." Now Laban had two daughters; the name of the older was Leah, and the name of the younger was Rachel. Leah had weak eyes, but Rachel was lovely in form, and beautiful. Jacob was in love with Rachel and said, "I'll work for you seven years in return for your younger daughter Rachel." Laban said, "It is better to give her to you than some other man. Stay here with me." So Jacob served seven years to get Rachel, but they seemed like only a few days to him because of

his love for her. Then Jacob said to Laban, "Give me my
wife. My time is completed, and I want to lie with her."
So Laban brought together all the people of the place
and gave a feast. But when evening came, he took his
daughter Leah and gave her to Jacob, and Jacob lay
with her. And Laban gave his servant girl Zilpah to his
daughter as her maidservant. When morning came,
there was Leah! (Gen. 29:13–25).

What a crafty man! It was typically Laban's style to
make agreements with Jacob and later to change their
meaning to suit his own interests. Here we see him
cheating Jacob of his desired bride after extracting seven
years' labor from his love-struck nephew. He passed
Leah off to Jacob in the manner of a dishonest busi-
nessman getting rid of damaged merchandise at full
price, which was exactly his attitude no matter what noble motives he might have claimed about the social awk-
wardness of a younger daughter marrying before the
elder one (Gen. 29:26). It really was of no concern to him
how Jacob or Leah or Rachel might have felt about his
deceitful tactics, nor what consequences might ensue for
the entire family. And there were plenty.

At first we are not told exactly how Leah felt about
being dumped on Jacob in this way. She may even have
been secretly pleased and hopeful that Jacob would accept her. But Jacob made no effort to hide his sense of
outrage: "What is this you have done to me? I served you
for Rachel, didn't I? Why have you deceived me?" (Gen.
29:15). How could Leah have failed to realize Jacob's bitter disappointment, or to feel deeply hurt by it? Although Jacob honorably fulfilled his obligation to Leah

by finishing out the bridal week with her (Laban had skillfully trapped him, and he had no real choice in the matter), it was obvious that he couldn't wait to gain the real desire of his heart. Finally, the week was over. "Jacob lay with Rachel also, and he loved Rachel more than Leah" (Gen. 29:30). Again, the fact was obvious to all, and most cruelly felt by Leah.

Sometimes it is hard for us to face facts. We try to see only what we want to see, instead of what is really there but unpleasant. The Talmud puts it thus: "We see things as we are, not as they are." We act as though our pretending a problem does not exist will make it go away, like the ostrich with his head buried in the sand. Or we devote ourselves to unraveling a marginal snag in our affairs rather than attacking the core of the difficulty. Much as she might have wished it otherwise, there was no physical remedy for Leah's weak eyes, and Jacob's preferential love for Rachel could not be altered. Leah had to learn to accept the facts of her situation before she could begin to live with them or grow by means of them. How have you faced the facts of your life?

## Confess Feelings

To accept the way things are and to admit that we might prefer them to be otherwise are two different matters. Our first clue to the way Leah handled her hurt feelings comes in Genesis 29:31: "When the LORD saw that Leah was not loved, he opened her womb, but Rachel was barren." Of course, we know that "nothing in all creation is hidden from God's sight. Everything is uncovered and laid bare before the eyes of him to whom we must give account" (Heb. 4:13).

God didn't need Leah to inform him of the facts, any more than he must depend on us for his omniscience today. We don't see Leah pouring out her feelings to the Lord in tearful vows either, as Hannah did in 1 Samuel 1. But we get the impression that Leah's relationship with God was steady and sustaining, so that he was tenderly aware of her situation and able to meet her needs with his sufficiency at every moment of tension. Leah's personality did not incline her to stir up hostility within the household; but she never could have withstood the pressures of her husband's disfavor and her sister's jealousy without knowing the constant comfort of communion with her God. Because she honestly expressed her desires before the Lord he was pleased to see, to listen, and to answer (Gen. 29:31–32, 30:17).

If we are examining Leah for her honest expression of feelings, we must explore the full range of her behavior. The passage concerning the mandrakes does not portray either of Jacob's wives in a very favorable light.

> During wheat harvest, Reuben went out into the fields and found some mandrake plants, which he brought to his mother Leah. Rachel said to Leah, "Please give me some of your son's mandrakes." But she said to her, "Wasn't it enough that you took away my husband? Will you take my son's mandrakes too?" "Very well," Rachel said, "he can sleep with you tonight in return for your son's mandrakes." So when Jacob came in from the fields that evening, Leah went out to meet him. "You must sleep with me," she said. "I have hired

you with my son's mandrakes." So he slept with her
that night (Gen. 38:14–16).

These verses give us a glimpse into what may have been
years of bitter rivalry between the sister-wives. The tension would truly have become intolerable had not Leah
taken refuge in God's love and blessing. Once again,
"God listened to Leah, and she became pregnant and
bore Jacob a fifth son" (Gen. 30:17). Rachel had to wait.

**Focus on God**

The course of Leah's steadfast devotion to God, the
secret of her survival, is best seen in those verses in
which she gives names to her sons and the sons of her
handmaid. Each of the names reflects the honest yearn-
ings of her heart, but always with renewed hope and
never in anger or bitterness. A chart will help us to see
the sequence and significance of these names, as Leah
continually chose to concentrate on her positive feelings
and her trust in God.

| Name | Translation | Verse |
|------|-------------|-------|
| *Reuben* (Gen. 29:32) | See a Son—sounds like Hebrew for, He has seen my misery. | "It is because the LORD has seen my misery. Surely my husband will love me now." |
| *Simeon* (Gen. 29:33) | One who hears | "Because the LORD has heard that I am not loved, he gave me this one too." |

101

| Levi (Gen. 29:34) | Attached | "Now at last my husband will become attached to me, because I have borne him three sons." |
| --- | --- | --- |
| **Judah** (Gen. 29:35) | Praise | "This time I will praise the LORD." |
| **Issachar** (Gen. 30:18) | Reward | "God has rewarded me for giving my maidservant to my husband." |
| **Zebulun** (Gen. 30:28) | Honor, or Dwelling Place | "God has presented me with a precious gift. This time my husband will treat me with honor, because I have borne him six sons." |

In contrast to these hope-filled meanings, the names that Rachel chose for the children of her maidservant and later for her own children reflect her spirit of discontent.

| **Name** | **Translation** | **Verse** |
| --- | --- | --- |
| **Dan** (Gen. 30:6) | He has Vindicated | "God has vindicated me; he has listened to my plea and given me a son." |
| **Naphtali** (Gen. 30:8) | My Struggle | "I have had a great struggle with my sister, and I have won." |
| **Joseph** (Gen. 30:24) | May He Add | "May the LORD add to me another son." |
| **Ben-Oni** (Gen. 35:18) | Son of My Trouble | |
| **Renamed Benjamin by Jacob** (Gen. 35:18) | Son of My Right Hand | |

When Leah countered Rachel's tactics by offering her servant Zilpah to Jacob, she still chose joyful names to express her hopes for the future rather than names that expressed her disappointments concerning the past.

| Name | Translation | Verse |
|------|-------------|-------|
| **Gad** (Gen. 30:11) | Good Fortune | "What good fortune!" |
| **Asher** (Gen. 30:13) | Happy | "How happy I am! The women will call me happy." |

### Fatal Favoritism

It would be nice to imagine that after the death of his beloved Rachel, Jacob came to have more appreciation of Leah's faithfulness. Unfortunately, there is no Bible verse that suggests such a happy ending to her story. Instead we find that just as Jacob preferred Rachel so he openly favored her two offspring, Joseph (Gen. 37:3) and Benjamin (Gen. 42:38 and 44:18–33), a bias that only served to exacerbate the jealous rivalry that already seethed within their home. In fact, the tragic consequences of playing favorites among one's children or wives are evident from the beginning to the end of Jacob's life.

This pattern leads us to consider two questions: How does Jacob's example challenge us to be more fair, if not equal, in our love and care for our children; and how can we find fulfillment if we live in homes where we do not receive the love we need and deserve, while someone or something else receives preferential treatment?

There is a folk rhyme that states,

> For every trouble under the sun,
>> There is an answer or there is none.
> If there be one, try to find it.
>> If there be none, never mind it.

Leah's situation in life did not drastically improve. In spite of her devotion to God she never gained the favor in her husband's eyes that Rachel enjoyed. Yet she seemed to achieve a contentment through her relationship with the Lord that her sister never attained. When we feel disappointed, hurt, or rejected because of a situation that we cannot change, we must learn what it is to persevere as Leah did. If we will face the facts, confess our feelings, and focus on God for strength and encouragement, we, too, can experience his precious comfort, even in the midst of unrelenting trials.

> Rejoice in the Lord always. I will say it again: Rejoice! Let your gentleness be evident to all. The Lord is near. Do not be anxious about anything, but in everything, by prayer and petition, with thanksgiving, present your requests to God. And the peace of God, which transcends all understanding, will guard your hearts and your minds in Christ Jesus (Phil. 4:4–7).

# PART THREE

# Women of Seduction

Delilah

Potiphar's Wife

Bathsheba

Delilah, Potiphar's wife, Bathsheba—do we really need three such questionable characters in our Bible study? Couldn't we just tiptoe past them lest we be tainted by association? Surely we don't need to know more about such a nasty subject as seduction; our tender ears and eyes might burn! Far be it from any of us even to know about such things, not to mention thinking of doing them, or at least getting caught.

But whether or not we need reminding of God's view of adultery, there are several broad principles each of us can apply to our lives as we study these three women. If we are honest, we may learn not so much about their seduction as about our own practice of deception, manipulation, and selfishness in pursuit of our desires. Pride will surface once more, as well as avarice and idleness, as root sins with which we have to deal.

The use of the word *seduction* in connection with these women does not necessarily assign blame either to them or to their partners for acts committed or attempted. Whether they actively seduced someone else or were themselves seduced is less significant than the intentions of their hearts, and of our own. The purpose of our investigation here will not be to determine which of these women were led astray and which did the leading, but rather to discover our motives and methods in relationship to the men with whom we live and work. May God direct us through our time of study and prayer to modify our behavior in ways that rightly reflect our relationship with him.

# 8

# Delilah

### Primary Scripture Reading

Judges 13–16

### Supplementary References

Matthew 26:14–16
John 3:30
1 John 2:16,17
1 Corinthians 13:4–8

### Questions for Study and Discussion

**1.** To which group of people did Delilah belong? What did the Philistine leaders offer her? Why? What was important to her besides money?

**2.** Review Samson's life story. List some of his strengths and weaknesses: physical, spiritual, intellectual, and emotional. Through which of his weaknesses was Delilah able to get the advantage over him?

**3.** How did Samson feel toward Delilah? Did she reciprocate his feelings? What opinion did Delilah have of Samson?

**4.** What three strategies did Delilah use to get Samson to tell her the secret of his strength? Why did he fall into her traps?

Where had he already heard the line "If you really loved me, you'd tell me"? Had he learned anything from his earlier experiences?

**5.** Have you ever resorted to nagging to get something you wanted? With what results? What sin is really at the root of this habit? How does Delilah's negative example encourage you to change your behavior in regard to other people?

**6.** Why did Delilah become so furious at Samson? Was she satisfied at the end of the story? What, do you think, happened to her after Samson was taken away?

**7.** What, if any, responsibility does Samson have for allowing Delilah to take advantage of him? How could he have acted with more faith in God and thus have avoided most of his misfortunes? What can you learn from his side of the story?

Delilah is probably the most notoriously wicked woman in the Bible, one with whom none of us would strive to identify. Why, then, do we need to concern ourselves with such an obviously poor model as we search the Old Testament to find God's principles for today's women? The unfortunate answer is that we may be more like her in character than we would care to admit. By examining her extremely negative case we may recognize several traits in ourselves that need to be confronted, confessed, and corrected.

Before delving into Delilah's character we must realize how important a part in her story was played by her lover Samson. She set the trap; he fell for it. Although we cannot fully explore Samson's personality within the pages of this study, we need to acknowledge the fact that the Spirit of God did "come upon him in power" at specific moments, but that He did not remain with him nor control his human passions all of the time. God enabled Samson to accomplish His judgment against the Philistines (Judg. 13:5, 14:4) and to lead Israel for twenty years (Judg. 16:31), but Samson was by no means a model of righteousness or moral strength for his people. Delilah's ability to subdue Samson's great physical strength was based on her exploitation of his intellectual and emotional weaknesses. By dividing her story, found in the Book of Judges, into three sections for exploration we may gain valuable insights for our own lives.

## Delilah's Desires

Delilah was motivated by one thing above all: money. When the Philistine rulers appealed to her to discover the secret of Samson's strength, they knew exactly what it would cost them to convince her. "See if you can lure [Samson] into showing you the secret of his great strength and how we can . . . subdue him. Each of us will give you eleven hundred shekels of silver" (Judg. 16:5). The starkness of their offer suggests that Delilah was accustomed to doing business of this kind. Although we cannot calculate the precise amount of the transaction in dollars, it is apparent that Delilah was satisfied with their contract and set about to earn the reward. Verse 18 of Judges 16 exposes her self-interest in all its simple ugliness: "When Delilah saw that he had told her everything, she sent word to the rulers of the Philistines, 'Come back once more; he has told me everything.' So the rulers of the Philistines returned with the silver in their hands." It is easy to imagine the scene in which Delilah carefully checked the weight of their coins before callously consummating her act of betrayal. (In the same way Judas Iscariot proved himself to be more concerned with his personal profit than with the person of God—see Matt. 26:14–16). Delilah seemed to have no misgivings as she proceeded to lull Samson to sleep, arranged to have his hair cut, and turned him over to the Philistine rulers, who gouged out his eyes and dragged him off to the prison grindstone. She may even have been in attendance later at the celebration feast honoring their god Dagon, when Samson was brought out to entertain the crowds and to carry out God's final judgment against them.

Throughout the biblical account it is quite apparent to the reader, if it was not to Samson, that Delilah had no tender thought or feeling for anyone but herself, and no desire other than to accomplish her own pecuniary objective. Samson's greatest mistake was in assuming that she was capable of reciprocating his love and that she could therefore be trusted with his most private and powerful secret.

Delilah's repeated berating of Samson reveals a secondary motivation for her actions. Her anger was kindled not so much because he had lied to her several times but because he had made a fool of her in front of the Philistines concealed in her room (Judg. 16:10, 13, 15). She obviously had no qualms about making a fool of him, but she was outraged at her failure to maintain her own image before the rulers. Not to deliver Samson into their hands meant loss of her reputation as well as of her reward. Samson's playful teasing was therefore a triple frustration to Delilah; pride and prestige were at stake in addition to personal profit.

110

After three unsuccessful attempts to seize Samson, the Philistines appeared to have lost confidence in Delilah, so they went back to their homes. When she finally learned the truth about Samson's vulnerability, she had to urge them, offering greater assurances, to return (Judg. 16:18). Delilah proved by her actions that she was more concerned about keeping the Philistines' trust than Samson's. She was willing to persevere to satisfy their interests and her own, without a single thought for his. Samson's obvious devotion to her could not swerve Delilah one degree from her selfish course.

Surely, no reader of this book is attracted to the brazenness of Delilah's treachery, but will you examine your own motives in light of her story? How much of your behavior is characterized by the need to achieve or maintain a good image in front of peers or superiors? The determination to save face is really a manifestation of self-pride, which is a serious sin (1 John 2:16). Do you allow your professional pursuit of profit and position to take precedence over personal loyalty to the people who are devoted to you? Do you safeguard or use to your own advantage the secrets someone has confided in you? Each one of us needs to acknowledge and find comfort in the fact that God has created us for a purpose, and that our best avenue to fulfillment is in striving to accomplish *his* will, not just in serving our own interests (1 John 2:17). "He must increase, I must decrease" (John 3:30, KJV). Proverbs 21:2 points the way to a larger perspective on our motives: "All a man's ways seem right to him, but the LORD weighs the heart." What will he find in your heart?

111

## Delilah's Demands

Delilah's repeated demand, "Tell me how you can be tied," is so blatant as nearly to fail the test of subterfuge, or even subtlety. If Samson had ever thought to ask her *why* she wanted to know his secret she might have been so bold as to tell him outright. We don't know how long he could have continued inventing sham answers to hold her at bay, or why he didn't guess her plot after she sounded the alarm for the third time: "Samson, the Philistines are upon you!" Frustrated, she abruptly switched her strategy in verse 15: "How can you say, 'I love you,' when you won't confide in me?" Because she neither loved nor trusted Samson, Delilah suspected that his need for privacy was equivalent to secrecy, which she equated with lack of love.

Have you ever said this to someone whose love for you is beyond question: "If you really loved me, you would . . ."? Were you not thereby trying to manipulate the other person into fulfilling your demands? This stratagem is one of the most dangerous and usually irrational ploys one can use to obtain one's own way. It is often effective, but almost always harmful to the would-be relationship.

Judges 16:16 gets to the heart of the matter of Delilah's methods: "With such nagging she prodded him day after day until he was tired to death." Samson was *literally* nagged to death! But how often, how relentlessly have I nagged my husband and my children, wearing them down until they have finally given in to my demands out of desperation to silence my voice. Let us all

112

take warning from Delilah's example, in this case her success rather than failure in achieving her goal.

Why do we resort to nagging, anyway? The habit is rooted, I think, not in any real concern for the other person's welfare, but in a basic lack of trust in his competence to make appropriate decisions either for himself or for others, especially when those decisions affect us. We readily take the role of self-appointed expert, badgering everyone else into complying with our orders, refusing to desist until we exhaust all opposition. "Do what I suggest because it is best for you" quickly degenerates into "Do what I say because it is best for me, and I won't stop reminding you until you give in." Basic selfishness is once again exposed for the ugly sin it is. Many of us, if we are honest, can identify such a nasty pattern operating in our households.

Overcoming the nagging habit is not easy, but it is possible. Honesty, prayer, and humor are the necessary ingredients to recovery. We must confess and resolve the fears that underlie our insecurities and lack of trust; we must allow God the liberty and power to communicate directly to each member of our families, not just through us; and we must accept our families' reminders of our relapses with humility and gratitude. When we focus on the sovereignty and love of God in every situation and for each of his children, our sense of inner peace is restored and our nagging tongues cease to wag. This approach can help us outgrow our bad habits.

Neither Delilah nor Samson knew the peace that passes understanding that comes as a fringe benefit of faith. Throughout his life Samson was motivated by a thirst for vengeance, another manifestation of selfishness. Delilah, too, was intent on getting whatever she could *for* herself, not giving *of* herself. She resorted to nagging and seduction as her most effective weapons in vanquishing Samson in order to obtain her own goal. Won't you give some thought now to your goals and weapons? Which of them are inconsistent with the cause of peace and need to be set aside? Put on, instead, the shield of faith and joy, and see the difference they make in your interpersonal relationships.

## Samson's Demise

Why did Samson fall for Delilah's trap and confide in her the secret of his unnatural strength? Apparently he was not as strong intellectually or emotionally as he was physically when the Lord came upon him in power. But the answer to the question is shockingly simple: he loved her. When she twisted his obvious love for her so it would work in opposition to his dedication to God as a Nazirite, he was utterly helpless to resist. She had found his most vulnerable point and applied unrelenting pressure upon it by nagging him "to death." She had no difficulty subduing his strength because she had wielded her best weapons against his greatest weakness, his love.

Let us now briefly consider the story from Samson's point of view. Long before he met Delilah, Samson had shown his susceptibility to physical beauty and sensual pleasure. His choice of a Philistine bride was patently based on her appearance alone (Judg. 14:1–7). In chapter 16 we are told that he spent a night with a prostitute.

Besides having an attraction to beauty Samson had a lack of resistance to nagging. His fiancée wept for seven days before his wedding in order to wrest from him the answer to his riddle, using almost the same words Delilah would employ later: "You hate me! You don't really love me. . . . you haven't told me . . ." (Judg. 14:16). Had Delilah researched his background before she planned her own strategy? Because her ultimate success depended upon his failures, her ability to pinpoint them was the key to her victory. Such a skilled markswoman had no difficulty hitting such an easy target.

Samson's infatuation with Delilah was the ultimate cause of his demise. Have you ever laid a "velvet trap" to catch a man's interest, or to further your own? Instead of rejoicing in your husband's devotion to you, have you ever turned it against him to obtain a purely selfish goal? Are you right now driving a knife into a heart that is laid bare with trust and love?

God's ideal, by which we must measure the quality of all love, is beautifully expressed in 1 Corinthians 13:4–8:

> Love is *patient*, love is *kind*. It does *not envy*, it does *not boast*, it is *not proud*. It is *not rude*, it is *not self-seeking*, it is *not easily angered*, it keeps no records of wrongs.
>
> Loves does *not delight in evil* but *rejoices with the truth*. It *always protects*, *always trusts*, *always hopes*, *always perseveres*. *Love never fails* (italics added).

Delilah's score on this test falls below zero.

She was impatient, unkind, envious, boastful, proud, rude, self-seeking, easily angered; she kept a record of wrongs committed against her, delighted in evil, resorted to subterfuge, failed to trust, failed to hope, failed completely. She did persevere, but in pursuit of selfish gain, not love. Consider these sixteen points in your life. How does your love measure up?

# 9

## Potiphar's Wife

### Primary Scripture Reading

Genesis 39

### Supplementary References

Genesis 37; 50:19–20
Psalm 42:5

### Questions for Study and Discussion

**1.** Follow the sequence of events in Genesis 37 by which Joseph came to serve in Potiphar's house. What was his position there initially? Was God punishing him or protecting him, do you think?

**2.** What qualities did Potiphar recognize in Joseph? What happened as a result? What did Potiphar's wife notice most about him? What do the differences in their interests suggest to you about the characters of Potiphar and his wife?

**3.** What did Potiphar's wife want from Joseph? What methods did she use to try to gain her objective? Did she offer Joseph anything in return? Do you detect any moral scruples or restraint in her behavior? How do you try to get other people to do what you want?

**4.** How did Joseph react to the advances of his master's wife? Why was his response likely quite a shock to Potiphar's wife? Was she used to such behavior? How did she respond? What sudden shift occurred in her strategy? Why?

**5.** Is there any significance to her keeping Joseph's cloak beside her until her husband came home (39:16)? What made Potiphar "burn with anger" (39:19)? Do you think anyone believed his wife's accusation? What might have happened otherwise?

**6.** In what ways was Joseph's faith in God a blessing while he was in Potiphar's house? How was it acknowledged by his heathen master and mistress? Can you think of an experience in your life in which the reality of your faith has been either appreciated or resented by unbelieving associates?

**7.** Do you think Potiphar's wife felt vindicated when Joseph was put in prison? How do you feel when your desires end in disappointment? What can you learn from Potiphar's wife about the evil effects of selfish manipulation? Instead of nursing your anger as she did, how can you focus on joy in every circumstance?

T he female half of the human race has often been referred to as the fair sex. There was nothing fair about Potiphar's wife. A mistress of manipulation, she put on deceit like one more gown, an outlet for her boredom and disappointment. As we focus on the role this heathen woman played in Joseph's inspiring biography, at least two observations emerge that can direct us to make necessary changes in the way we regard other people.

## Opportunities—To Share or To Shun

Sold into slavery by his jealous brothers, Joseph entered Egypt on the lowest rung of the social ladder. But whether he experienced adversity or prosperity in the following years, God's powerful protection and purpose for his life were always affirmed. While God blessed Joseph, people around him usually noticed some benefits to themselves as well.

> The LORD *was with Joseph and he prospered,* and he lived in the house of his Egyptian master. When *his master saw that the LORD was with him and that the LORD gave him success in everything he did, Joseph found favor in his eyes* and became his attendant. Potiphar put him in charge of his household, and he entrusted to his care everything he owned. From the time he put him in charge of his household and of all that he owned, *the LORD blessed the household of the Egyptian because of Joseph. The blessing of the LORD was on everything Potiphar had, both in the house and in the field.* So he left in Joseph's care everything he had; with Joseph in charge, he did not concern himself with anything except the food he ate (Gen. 39:2–6, italics added).

All three of his superiors in Egypt—first Potiphar and later the prison warden and the pharaoh—were quick to appreciate the skill and satisfaction that surrounded Joseph and to put him in charge of all their affairs (Gen. 39:4, 22; 41:41). Thus, Joseph spread the goodness of God through his successful service in Egypt. But at the same time, there was one opportunity he had to shun.

Attracted to the young, handsome, and successful overseer who had brought much prosperity to her household, Potiphar's wife was determined to enjoy a portion of the abundance for herself. With her husband devoting his attention only to the food he ate (Gen. 39:6), this affluent aristocrat was apparently lonely or bored enough to "cast her eyes upon Joseph" (Gen. 39:7, KJV) as a most likely source of entertainment. She was not flirting but flaunting her power when she demanded, "Come to bed with me." Clearly, no moral considerations or religious convictions arose to slow down her headlong pursuit of Joseph; neither did the possibility of a refusal on his part occur to her.

Is there someone who finds favor in your eyes because of God's blessing on him or her in the way that Joseph found favor with the Egyptian officials; or do you cast your eyes upon that person for your selfish pleasure, as did Potiphar's wife? (See Matt. 5:29 for Christ's solution to this problem.)

Before we sit in judgment on the behavior of this pagan woman, however, we should ask ourselves whether our own behaviors or attitudes are really any better. To what extent are you considerate of the needs of others? What tactics do you use to get people to do what *you* want? Perhaps your objective is not the same as that of Potiphar's wife, but how different are your methods? Do you tease, scream, or sulk? Do you make threats or false promises? What is your definition of manipulation, and would you fit the category of an individual who tries to use other people to satisfy your desires, regardless of their desires? How would your associates answer this question about you?

Joseph's ability to resist Potiphar's wife is all the more impressive when we consider the many favorable circumstances that might have led him to accept her proposition. Hadn't Joseph worked hard for his Egyptian master? Could he not presume that Potiphar's wife was just one more evidence of God's blessing, a bonus dropped into his lap (literally!) to encourage him in his period of slavery? How *are* we to know which situations are allowed as God's will, and which are to be avoided as Satan's temptations? Joseph was held in check by two considerations that may help us to determine the answers to these questions when they arise in our lives.

> But he refused. "With me in charge," he told her, "my master does not concern himself with anything in the house; everything he owns he has entrusted to my care. No one is greater in this house than I am. My master has withheld nothing from me except you, because you are his wife. How then could I do such a wicked thing and sin against God?" (Gen. 39:8–9).

Joseph refused her, but not merely out of consideration for his own status or personal safety. The possibility of getting caught and suffering for his offense were beside the point. He simply explained that he could not violate either his master's trust or his own faith in God, the two solid principles by which he evaluated every other aspect and issue in his life. He valued his personal relationship with God more highly than his personal pleasure; in fact, it was the source of all his pleasure, and he knew it! Experiencing such satisfaction in his Lord, he had no desire to jeopardize this fellowship by satisfying

121

the sinful demands of Potiphar's wife. Although he did not have the whole revelation of God found in the completed Scriptures as we do, Joseph understood that God's blessing derives as much from God's holiness as from his love, and that he demands righteous conduct as much as appreciation in response to his gifts. When God had already been so good to him, how could Joseph be so ungrateful as to pluck the one fruit that had been forbidden? His choice was clear.

Perhaps you feel that you are a victim of circumstances, just a pawn on the chessboard of life, with few or no opportunities for independent or meaningful action. You seem to move forward one slow square at a time, whatever the interplay of events around you, feeling no effect and having none. The King James Version uses the expression *and it came to pass* eight times in this thirty-ninth chapter of Genesis. Do things just "come to pass" in your life, without any seeming control or purpose on your part? Are you helpless in the face of circumstances, or is there some way to identify the one significant and fruitful course intended by God for you?

Joseph relied on his knowledge of God's character both as an anchor to hold him fast to God's will and as a rudder to guide him safely through the rough waters of temptation. We, too, can hold fast to God and apply the reality of his character and promises to our present situation when we study his Word, and then pray for his will to be made clearer. We also need the desire and the strength to make the right choice. The Holy Spirit promises to guide us with an inner sense of "peace that transcends all understanding" (Phil. 4:7) when we truly desire to walk with him. Rather than becoming confused

by the pressures of conflicting or compromising pos-
sibilities, we can be assured, as Joseph was, that God's
commands are never superseded by circumstances as
indicators of his will.

So Joseph refused. He also did another wise thing—
he put some distance between himself and the temptress. Genesis 39:10 states, "And though she spoke to
Joseph day after day, he refused to go to bed with her or
even be with her." No amount of nagging or alluring
could prevail against such fortitude and faith. When
opportunity knocked, Joseph locked the door tightly
against temptation.

## Outrage or Outreach?

Do you remember the safety rule, Stop, look, listen
before you step out into traffic? Potiphar's wife certainly
stopped and looked, but she wouldn't listen. Although
Joseph found the strength to say no, Potiphar's wife
would not take no for an answer. She only redoubled her
efforts to gain the object of her lust. Perhaps she even
resorted to some behind-the-scenes manipulations to set
her best snare for the overseer.

> One day he went into the house to attend to his duties,
> and none of the household servants was inside. She
> caught him by his cloak and said, "Come to bed with
> me!" But he left his cloak in her hand and ran out of the
> house (Gen. 39:11–12).

Can't you just imagine Potiphar's wife dismissing all the
domestic servants, contriving some business for Joseph

that would compel him to come into the house, and then pouncing on him from behind the door? What may have begun as a passing fancy had developed into a burning passion when her advances were repeatedly spurned— the thing she wanted most was the one thing she couldn't have. How furious she must have been when Joseph slipped from her clutches and ran, leaving his cloak hanging limply in her hands! She was both bitterly disappointed and deeply offended. No wonder she kept that cloak beside her all day as she nursed her feelings of outrage.

Have you ever felt like saying to yourself, "Well, if I can't have thus and so, at least I'll make sure that no one else can enjoy it"? It is said that to the victor go the spoils, but for those who can't be victors the role of spoiler is almost as satisfying at times. Such people don't seem to mind losing if they can bring someone else down to the bottom of the heap with them. They seem determined to destroy what they can't have for themselves. It's not a very mature response to failure, but it certainly is a human one, and it is exactly the way Potiphar's wife reacted. She quickly thought, "If I can't win with plan A, I'll switch to plan B, using the evidence of this cloak *against* Joseph to prove my power over him for punishment, if not for pleasure." Notice the wording of Genesis 39:13–18:

> When she saw that he had left his cloak in her hand and had run out of the house, she called her household servants. "Look," she said to them, "this Hebrew has been brought to us to make sport of us! He came in here to sleep with me, but I screamed. When he heard

me scream for help, he left his cloak beside me and ran out of the house." She kept his cloak beside her until his master came home. Then she told him this story: "That Hebrew slave you brought us came to me to make sport of me. But as soon as I screamed for help, he left his cloak beside me and ran out of the house."

Of course, Potiphar's wife was making more sport with Joseph in her accusation than he ever dreamed of trying to make with her. It almost seems that she became more convinced of her story with each retelling. We sense her twisted delight as she kept the cloak beside her until she could repeat her fantasy for her husband. To her, revenge could be almost as sweet as the sexual pleasure she had anticipated.

Did Potiphar believe his wife's deception? Verses 19–20 tell us, "When his master heard the story his wife told him, saying, 'This is how your slave treated me,' he burned with anger. Joseph's master took him and put him in prison, the place where the king's prisoners were confined." Apparently there was no investigation of the charge against Joseph, although it would have been interesting to know whether the household servants would testify to hearing screams. Clearly, Potiphar was angry, but with whom? He had to take some action, but how severe?

If Potiphar really thought that Joseph had betrayed his trust and violated his wife, surely he could have sold, beaten, or even killed his slave for such an outrageous deed. Instead, Joseph's imprisonment among the king's prisoners seems more of a protection than a punishment. Perhaps Potiphar's anger was prompted as much by regret that his wife's behavior had necessitated the loss of a good overseer as by real belief in her accusation.

God continued to be with Joseph in prison, and he rose to a new position of responsibility. Joseph acknowledged God's help when he interpreted dreams for the cupbearer, the baker, and finally the king. After he had risen to power in Egypt and revealed his identity to his brothers, Joseph told them, "But God sent me ahead of you to preserve for you a remnant on earth and to save your lives by a great deliverance. So, then, it was not you who sent me here, but God" (Gen. 45:7–8).

After their father's death, Joseph reassured his brothers with words that could as well have been addressed to Potiphar's wife: "Am I in the place of God? You intended to harm me, but God intended it for good to accomplish what is now being done, the saving of many lives" (Gen. 50:19–20). The harm intended by Potiphar's wife turned out for good also. Her outrage led to Joseph's opportunities for outreach, for he continued to spread God's truth and goodness wherever he was, until God had accomplished his full purpose for Joseph's life.

How do we deal with disappointments? What is disappointment, anyway? Perhaps we can recognize in this feeling, as in our fears, a signal of a soft spot in our shield of faith, a place where we still want to follow our own way—to trust in our own efforts and abilities to manipulate others—rather than to submit wholeheartedly to God's purposes. It is only when we give up our selfish goals and seek what God desires for us and through us that we can marvel at and enjoy his plan no matter what its temporary personal impact may be.

Will you now choose to consider your disappointments as God's appointments, trusting him to know and to do what is best? In the strength of his joy (see Neh. 8:10) we can, instead of seeking solace in subterfuge and seduction to soothe our hurts, rejoice in righteousness. As David said:

> Why are you downcast, O my soul?
>   Why so disturbed within me?
> Put your hope in God,
>   for I will yet praise him,
>   my Savior and my God.
>
> (Ps. 42:5)

# 10

## Bathsheba

### Primary Scripture Reading

2 Samuel 11, 12; 1 Kings 1

### Supplementary References

Psalm 26:11–12
Proverbs 26:23–27
John 8:32; 14:6
1 John 1:5–9

### Questions for Study and Discussion

**1.** As you read Bathsheba's story, try to sort out the roles of the four leading men in her life: David, Uriah, Nathan, and Solomon. Chart, if you can, the influence of each one on her life, and her relationship with each.

**2.** What was Bathsheba doing on her rooftop? Was she aware of her lack of privacy? Was she deliberately tempting the king to sin, do you think?

**3.** When the messengers from the palace came to her door, what options did Bathsheba have? Read 2 Sam. 11:3–4 in several translations, if you can. Do you think that Bathsheba was forced to submit to David or that she willingly accepted and aroused his attention? Was she a seductress or a "seducee"?

**4.** What did Bathsheba do next? What did David do about her predicament? How would the situation have been different if Uriah the Hittite had returned to his home when David summoned him? Do you think Bathsheba was informed of David's plots concerning her husband?

**5.** How was David made aware of his sin? What did he do about it? What did God promise him? How was Bathsheba blessed after her great loss?

**6.** Later in her life (1 Kings 1) Bathsheba and Nathan interceded with David to declare Solomon heir to the throne. Do you find any wrongdoing on their part in that instance? Does Bathsheba's conduct in that chapter give any further insight into her personality as it was first revealed in 2 Samuel 11?

**7.** How much of the truth do you admit to yourself and to others? Are there aspects of either your present or your past life that you feel you need to conceal from others? Who would be hurt by your full disclosures? How much does God know about you? How could you restore your relationship with God and with other people to be more open and honest than it is now?

Do you remember the seventh commandment? "Thou shalt not commit adultery" (Exod. 20:14). In our day, violations of God's design for sex within marriage seem commonplace in every newspaper and neighborhood. Infidelity (sexual and otherwise) is disguised and dignified with many euphemisms, while marital faithfulness is downgraded as an old-fashioned if not already obsolete phenomenon. In the Bible one of the most notorious examples of adultery involved Bathsheba, whose complex character and circumstances seem remarkably contemporary. From the glimpse into her personality that Scripture allows us we can deepen our insights into our own concept and practice of integrity, and balance this study of subterfuge and seduction.

It is said that beauty is only skin deep, but for Bathsheba skin-deep was enough to get her into more hot water than filled her rooftop tub. The bare facts of her case seem clear enough. What is far more difficult is to determine the proper allotment of responsibility for what happened. The text in 2 Samuel 11 has been diversely interpreted to substantiate almost every view of women held through the centuries: their power and their weakness; their innocence and their craftiness; their strength and their vulnerability. Can we hope to uncover the real Bathsheba beneath the layers of bias that have been wrapped around her?

We shall consider Bathsheba's story in relation to the four men who played prominent roles in her life: David, Uriah, Joab, and Nathan. Much of her character comes to light as we analyze the impact of each of these men. We are also helped by the opportunity to view Bathsheba in different episodes of her life, from her introduction to David, through her intercession for Solomon, and finally in her involvement with Adonijah's insurrection. Still, some important questions cannot be answered directly from the text alone. However, we can learn many critical lessons as we examine our own hearts and ask God once again to apply his Word to our lives.

## Leading Men

The account in 2 Samuel 11 focuses on King David. Indeed, if he had not been intimately involved, Bathsheba's story would seem much less significant to us, though not, of course, to God. David had been described as a "man after God's own heart" (1 Sam. 13:14), who was anointed king after Saul proved his disobedience and indifference to God's commands. Yet, here we see David at his worst. How could God favor such a sinner with his friendship? By his grace God appreciated David for his attitude, not his actions (1 Sam. 16:7), just as he reckons us perfected in Christ through faith, not through our own achievements.

In tracing the sequence of events that led to the murder of Uriah the Hittite we find a hint of warning even in the apparent simplicity and ordinariness of the first scene. "In the spring, at the time when kings go off to war, David sent Joab out with the king's men and the whole Israelite army. They destroyed the Ammonites and besieged Rabbah. But David remained in Jerusalem" (2 Sam. 11:1). In short, David was suffering from an acute case of spring fever. Although he probably had no premeditated plan to seduce a soldier's wife, he was ripe for trouble from the outset. When Bathsheba appeared on her rooftop to bathe, fully visible from the palace balcony, David naturally stopped pacing and stayed to enjoy the view. He was sufficiently aroused to inquire after this beautiful woman; he sent messengers to bring her to the palace where he slept with her.

Soon afterward Bathsheba notified David that she was pregnant. He made no effort to disavow his part in her predicament, but neither did he respond uprightly. First he summoned Uriah, Bathsheba's husband, to return from the field, hoping that the soldier would visit his own home and bed while in Jerusalem. When that ruse failed, David ordered Uriah placed at the front of the battlelines to be killed by the enemy.

For his part, Uriah affirmed his loyalty to the king by refusing to sleep with his own wife while his fellow soldiers remained on duty in the field (although David had obviously not exhibited any loyalty towards *him* in this regard). He never guessed that his reputation and his very life were in jeopardy. Even after David made him drunk on his second night in town, Uriah resisted the inclination to go home.

Would Bathsheba have concealed the truth from her husband if he *had* come to her? The answer to this question, if we could get it, might help us to determine the extent of her guilt—if she had deliberately enticed the king, we might expect her to deceive her husband as well. Since Uriah did not go home, we may turn the question from one of speculation about Bathsheba to introspection: What is *my* integrity index? How honest am *I* to express the whole truth of my most intimate actions and feelings to my spouse, parents, children, friends, or colleagues?

Whether or not we attempt to conceal the truth from those with whom we live and work, "everything is uncovered and laid bare before the eyes of him to whom we must give account" (Heb. 4:13). What truth do we try to hide when we think someone else wouldn't understand? Isn't it really that we want to protect our egos and avoid dealing with our sins? We have no need to fear the opinions of other people when we realize that God already knows the whole truth about us.

> God is light; in him there is no darkness at all. If we
> claim to have fellowship with him yet walk in dark-

ness, we lie and do not live by the truth. . . . If we confess our sins, he is faithful and just and will forgive us our sins and purify us from all unrighteousness (1 John 1:5–9).

The axiom "What he doesn't know won't hurt him" certainly wasn't true for Uriah. In his case what he didn't know killed him! Deceit is injurious, possibly even fatal, to us and to others. Even if we don't actually commit murder, it is easy enough to kill a relationship or alienate ourselves from God by failing to be honest. We have no need to resort to such subterfuge when we comprehend the mercy and all-seeing power of our loving God.

We find another lesson concerning the effect of sin when we consider Joab's role in this story. As field general in the campaign against the Ammonites he received David's orders to place Uriah in the front ranks to be killed. Joab obliged the king, but he did not fail to make use of the significance of this favor to cover his own losses in the battle (see 2 Sam. 11:18–24). Joab's loss of esteem for King David, which culminated in treason, seems to have had its origin in this incident (compare 2 Sam. 11:19–21 with 2 Sam. 12:27–28 and 1 Kings 1:7).

Similarly, our handling (upright or otherwise) of certain individuals or situations may touch other lives and circumstances far removed from our immediate intentions, like the ripples that move across a pond from the splash of a single stone. When the "man after God's own heart" fell, many others tumbled with him. Will you ask God to deal with your sin now, so that your relationship with him may be expressed, not contradicted, in all your relationships with other people?

"But the thing David had done displeased the LORD" (2 Sam. 11:27). God dispatched the prophet Nathan to confront and rebuke David, who confessed his sin, repented, and accepted first the Lord's punishment and then his full forgiveness (2 Sam. 12:14, 25; also read Ps. 51 with this background in mind). As we shall see, Nathan later joined Bathsheba to insure Solomon's ascension to the throne. Thus, Nathan delivered the Lord's rebuke but later served as his agent of restoration. He was uncompromising toward the sin of adultery but flexible in his relationship with the individuals involved. Nathan's life was so dedicated to God's service that God used him to accomplish his purposes in the lives of people who at one time offended but later glorified his name. Both David and Bathsheba responded to the straightforwardness of Nathan's message by recommitting themselves to God's will.

Could God ever use you as a Nathan to rebuke a sin and at the same time to show such love that the sinner's relationship with God is restored? How have you responded to God's call to repentance and revival when it was expressed through a Nathan whom he had sent into your life?

## Leading Lady, or Misleading?

We've looked at the influence of four men on Bathsheba's life. What was her side of the story? The biblical record is quite brief, and evidently written from King David's perspective. Bathsheba's feelings and the full facts of the case from her point of view are not recorded.

135

A further difficulty is that various English translations allow for slightly different interpretations of her role in the whole affair. For example, the King James Version states, "And David sent messengers and *took* her; and she came in unto him, and he lay with her" (2 Sam. 11:4). From this wording we might conclude that Bathsheba was helpless to resist the king's command or the messengers' enforcement of his desire; David summoned her to the royal bed, and she had no choice but to submit to the humiliating ordeal. The New International Version leaves us more room to wonder: "Then David sent messengers to *get* her. She came to him and he slept with her." Here we might understand that Bathsheba had somewhat more choice in the matter, and perhaps was more willing to come, but how much? Could she have refused the invitation? Perhaps she did not realize the king's intentions at first. But what were *her* intentions in bathing on the rooftop in the first place; or had she at least considered the possible outcomes? If she assumed that all the fighting men were on duty in the field along with her husband, she may have felt quite secure in bathing in the cool and quiet of her rooftop, the equivalent of a private courtyard. But surely the palace dominated the skyline above her. It must have been common knowledge that David had remained in Jerusalem. Was she aware of the king's attention, and was she trying to arouse his interest? Had Bathsheba seduced the king in fact? Did David invade her privacy or fall into her trap? Was Bathsheba a naive housewife or a scheming temptress—victim or a vixen?

Volumes have been written trying to resolve these questions according to the various preferences of the authors. Each reader must come to his own or her own conclusions. The value of the biblical account lies as much in its revelation of our own hearts as in its historical veracity (though we can trust its truthfulness for both objectives). Do you ever see yourself in the role of temptress or "temptee"? Are you aware of the extent of your attraction and attractiveness to members of the opposite" sex at certain times and places? Do you take steps either to exploit or protect others by your response to these feelings?

Sexual stimulation is not sinful in itself; it is basic to our natures as God's created beings. However, sexual activity outside of marriage is expressly forbidden by God, no matter how many people we could point to in the Bible or in contemporary life as negative examples. In this area are you careful to maintain your feet on level ground, alert to possible pitfalls so that neither you nor others are caused to stumble (Ps. 26:11–12; Prov. 26:23–27)?

In what other ways does Bathsheba's story challenge us? Our insight into her character deepens when we examine some of the passages relating other incidents in her life following her act of adultery. She seems to emerge a stronger personality as the story unfolds. Second Samuel 11:5 states, "The woman conceived and sent word to David, saying 'I am pregnant.'" This statement suggests that Bathsheba was not promiscuous in extramarital affairs. Her desperation is revealed in the very terseness of her message. She employed no subterfuge or deceit here; the cold, bold truth illuminates a basic honesty in Bathsheba, which David, her partner, failed to exhibit at this point. He took matters into his own hands, first to recall Uriah and then to order his certain death. The fact that Bathsheba is not mentioned during these maneuvers implies that she may have been innocent of the details of David's dealings first with Uriah and then with Joab in response to the message indicating she was pregnant. Likewise, we may believe that Bathsheba's mourning over the death of her husband was sincere, and perhaps intensified if she harbored any feelings of guilt over her part in the act that betrayed him (2 Sam. 11:26).

We have suggested honesty, innocence, and sincerity as at least part-time qualities manifested in Bathsheba's character. Even so, she seems not to have resisted the opportunity to sin when the occasion presented itself. She turned away from trust in God to reliance on her own resources and the power of the king. The lesson was costly.

Of course, David's marrying Bathsheba after committing adultery and murder was the honorable thing to do in a sense, but it did not resolve the basic issue of sin, nor did it help to settle David's domestic affairs. Confession and repentance were still necessary to restore David to an open and effective relationship with the Lord. God's mercy and love were evident, along with his righteous judgment, in allowing the child conceived in sin to die. Bathsheba obviously suffered as much as David over this great loss.

New life was born of David's and Bathsheba's grief, and God sent word through Nathan that the second child, Solomon, should also carry the name Jedidiah, which means "loved by the LORD" (2 Sam. 12:24–25). God's full forgiveness and David's complete return to health and power are indicated at the close of 2 Samuel 12 by David's defeat of the Ammonites.

## Leading Questions

The remaining chapters of 2 Samuel record various incidents of friction and bloodshed among members of David's household and throughout the nation. Sons and daughters from different marriages committed incest, murder, and rebellion in defiance of their father's authority. Bathsheba and her offspring are not mentioned again until 1 Kings 1. By that time David was quite old; he had great difficulty maintaining his body temperature, not to mention his kingdom. Adonijah, another of David's sons, had gained the support of several of David's civil leaders and was attempting to claim the throne of his father for himself.

Nathan the prophet informed Bathsheba of Adonijah's conspiracy and instructed her concerning the best approach to take.

> Go in to King David and say to him, "My Lord the king, did you not swear to me your servant: 'Surely Solomon your son shall be king after me, and he will sit on my throne'? Why then has Adonijah become king?" While you are still talking to the king, I will come in and confirm what you have said (1 Kings 1:13–14).

The two performed their roles perfectly and obtained the desired response from David.

139

> The king took an oath: "As surely as the LORD lives,
> who has delivered me out of every trouble, I will
> surely carry out today what I swore to you by the
> LORD, the God of Israel: Solomon your son shall be
> king after me, and he will sit on my throne in my
> place" (1 Kings 1:29–30).

Solomon was forthwith officially proclaimed king, even as Adonijah was finishing the feast he had served in honor of his own false claim. Solomon's first act as king was to spare Adonijah's life, although he punished the other conspirators according to David's instructions (1 Kings 2).

At first glance Nathan's and Bathsheba's behavior in 1 Kings 1 may appear to be a conspiracy. The elements of secrecy, urgency, and careful rehearsal of strategy were all present in their actions. On the other hand, the oath of which David was reminded, in which he had named Solomon as his successor, is not recorded in Scripture. Can we know for certain whether Bathsheba and Nathan were simply jogging the king's memory for the cause of justice or were subtly twisting it for selfish purposes?

We do have several clues to help us believe the rightness of their cause and conduct in this instance. First, we have no reason to doubt Nathan's integrity in serving God by accurately communicating his word. It was his information and insight that prompted Bathsheba to approach David on her son's behalf. Second, there is no indication of guile or false representation of the facts. Bathsheba's confidence in her appeal seems to have been based on its truth, not on her prejudices or her power to seduce the king one more time. Third, it is not very likely that the old, cold king could have been roused to action so quickly had not the facts and motives of the case been correctly perceived and presented. And finally, the record of Solomon's accession in 1 Chronicles 28–29 omits any mention of legitimate dissent, which tends to uphold the appropriateness of Bathsheba's and Nathan's efforts to place Solomon on the throne as rightful heir.

Once again, this incident demonstrates several favorable qualities in Bathsheba's character, such as her loyalty and forthrightness. It also throws some light on her personality and behavior back in the scene on the rooftop. If we approve of her courage and confidence in approaching the king as an offended mother in this passage, we must recognize her basic strength of character; then we cannot altogether excuse as naive, weak, or innocent her earlier behavior.

However, we are beginning to see this lady not as a shallow black-and-white figure, but as a real, complex human being. She appears more realistically when we recognize her alternately sinful and honorable desires, the fluctuations between tragedy and triumph in her life. Can you identify in any way with Bathsheba's struggles to sort out and follow the path of truth while battling wicked plots both outside and within herself?

One more incident shows us what may be the end result of such conflict. Soon after David's death Adonijah approached Bathsheba to ask for a special favor.

"As you know," he said, "the kingdom was mine. All Israel looked to me as their king. But things changed, and the kingdom has gone to my brother; for it has come to him from the LORD. Now I have one request to

141

> make of you. . . . Please ask King Solomon—he will
> not refuse you—to give me Abishag the Shunammite
> as my wife" (1 Kings 2:15–18).

This request may sound duly polite and pious to our ears, but Solomon detected trouble and refused to grant his mother this favor, even though he had already promised not to turn her down (v. 20). He smelled treason, whereas Bathsheba probably had hoped to achieve some measure of reconciliation between the two half-brothers. She who may have resorted to subterfuge earlier in her life thus became an unwitting partner in a stratagem against her own son. She had always found the line between honesty and deceit fuzzy and was now no closer to clarity.

Fortunately, Solomon was not taken in by Adonijah's plot. He took decisive action to squelch the rebellion and to solidify his own power to rule. He had learned to rely on the wise and understanding heart he had received from God and not on the advice of his counselors, not even his own mother.

To the question "What is truth?" Christ gave Pontius Pilate the answer, "I am the way and the truth and the life. No one comes to the Father except through me" (John 14:6). He also said, "You will know the truth, and the truth will set you free" (John 8:32).

When you know Christ the truth, there is no need to get tangled up in false strategies and seductions. When you trust yourself to his way, you need not resort to cunning to gain your own way. When his life is in you, you can safely yield your life and your children's lives to his tender care, instead of having to plan for your own safety.

If we are honest, we may detect several similarities between Bathsheba's character and circumstances in our own lives. None of us lives perfectly; sin is real and powerful for everyone. But it does not have to be the end of the story for Bathsheba or for us. There is a way out. The path to freedom—freedom from sin and from subterfuge and from self—lies through Christ the truth. Do you know him? Are you free?

# PART FOUR

# Women of Hospitality and Service

Widow of Zarephath
Deborah, Keturah, and Abishag
Rahab

It is not who we are and what we have that matter to God when he evaluates the quality of our service. "Inasmuch as ye have done it unto one of the least of these my brethren, ye have done it unto me," Christ said (Matt. 25:40, KJV). He might also have said, "You were among the least of these my sisters and had nothing, yet all that you gave and did for me shall be richly rewarded in heaven." In this section of the book we can discover Christ's promise and the privilege of serving God and humanity unselfishly by looking at some lovely, lowly souls whose generous spirits brought them to the highest ranks on God's honor roll.

A dying widow, a nursemaid, an old man's wife, a bed warmer, and a prostitute are accurate but not very impressive descriptions of the five women we consider now. Their names are not nearly as familiar to us as those of the people whom they served—Joshua, Elijah, Rebekah, Abraham, and David. But they were giants in their own right. They offered themselves to the Lord and were blessed because they put their faith to work and learned the faithfulness of God in sustaining his true servants.

In the New Testament the disciples needed to understand Jesus' principles and his example of service.

> Jesus called them together and said, "You know that the rulers of the Gentiles lord it over them, and their high officials exercise authority over them. Not so with you. Instead, whoever wants to become great among you must be your servant, and whoever wants to be first must be your slave—just as the Son of Man did not come to be served, but to serve, and to give his life as a ransom for many" (Matt. 20:25–28).

Notice that Jesus does not say it was wrong to want to be number one. He even tells us how to do it. If we would succeed in this endeavor, a good place to begin would be to apply the models of hospitality and service provided by these Old Testament women.

# 11

## Widow of Zarephath

### Primary Scripture Reading

1 Kings 16, 17

### Supplementary References

Luke 4:25, 26
Mark 12:41–44
Philippians 4:11, 12
1 Peter 4:9–11
Hebrews 12:2–11

### Questions for Study and Discussion

**1.** Who was the king of Israel during Elijah's lifetime? How did he provoke God's anger? How was Elijah sustained at the beginning of the drought? Why did God send him to Zarephath? How far was this city from Elijah's home region of Gilead?

**2.** What did God tell Elijah about the woman? Was she similarly prepared to receive and sustain him, do you think? At the time of their first meeting, what was she doing?

**3.** How did the widow react to Elijah's requests? What two hard things did he ask of her? What promise did he make? Were there any conditions to the promise? How well did she meet the requirements? Was the promise kept? What principle of giving do you find in verses 13 and 14 of chapter 17?

**4.** What happened that caused the widow to turn against Elijah? What did he do? Why didn't the woman herself pray to God? What did God do in answer to Elijah's prayers? What did the woman do in response? How do you know that "the word of the Lord . . . is the truth"?

**5.** What does this passage suggest about the quality, as opposed to the quantity, of the hospitality we offer to others? How is it related to the story of the widow in Mark 12:41–44?

**6.** How did God's provision for Elijah during the famine prepare the prophet for his later victory at Carmel in 1 Kings 18? In what ways was the widow blessed for her service?

**7.** What is the point of Christ's use of the widow's story in Luke 4? How does her example stir your heart to be available for God's service? What do a person's family background or credentials have to do with being appointed by God?

The story of the widow of Zarephath teaches us that hospitality is as much a matter of attitude as outward expression. Unlike Rahab, who used her protection of Joshua's spies as a bargaining tool to achieve her deliverance, this nameless lady displayed no ulterior motives and no desire to attract the attention of her guest, who had to solicit her help. Although she did not immediately offer to share her home and her last meal with the prophet Elijah, her believing response to his assurances of God's provision challenges us today to consider how clearly our demonstrations of hospitality reflect the depth of our faith.

## Fertile for Faith

To understand the widow's situation in its context, we need to begin with the events of 1 Kings 17. Elijah had prophesied to King Ahab that God would send a famine to Israel in judgment of its evil. For three and one-half years no rain fell and food was scarce. During that time God had ordered Elijah to stay near the brook at Kerith, where ravens brought him food each morning and evening (1 Kings 17:1–6); but eventually the brook dried up. Then God told Elijah, "Go at once to Zarephath of Sidon and stay there. I have commanded a widow in that place to supply you with food (*sustain thee* in KJV)" (1 Kings 17:9).

This widow seemed totally unprepared to receive her guest, despite the fact that God had specifically informed Elijah that he had commanded her. She had very little to offer. Apparently God had selected her more for what he desired to do in her life than for what she could do for his prophet, and he had more suitably prepared her heart than her home for hospitality. Elijah even had to ask her for the basic courtesy of getting him some water, which she was willing enough to bring from the nearby well. But when he asked her to bring him a piece of bread as well, she had to confess that she was destitute and had none at all to give him. In fact, she said, her situation was so bad that only a little flour remained. "I am gathering two sticks, that I may go in and dress it for me and my son, that we may eat it, and die" (1 Kings 17:12, KJV).

Two things are important to notice about this widow. First, she had nothing to give Elijah; and second, she lived in Zarephath of Sidon. This was the homeland of Queen Jezebel, who was directly responsible for leading Ahab and all Israel into the idolatry and wickedness for which the nation was being punished at the time (1 Kings 16:3). What less likely place of refuge for Elijah could be imagined, either by him (who would have viewed Sidon as enemy territory) or by the widow (a starving pagan woman)? We must look beneath the superficial unlikelihood of such a coupling to discover God's deeper wisdom in discerning the hearts of his chosen servants. In fact, Jesus Christ used this very pair as an example of this point when he said:

> "I assure you that there were many widows in Israel in Elijah's time, when the sky was shut for three and a half years and there was a severe famine throughout the land. Yet Elijah was not sent to any of them, but to a widow in Zarephath in the region of Sidon" (Luke 4:25–26).

Surely this poor pagan widow could not have suspected that she was appointed by the Lord Jehovah to sustain his prophet; yet, her humblest gesture provided the fertile soil in which her faith could grow. God intended an even greater purpose—to minister to her needs as well and thereby reveal himself in a special way to her and to all who read her story.

Having met the widow and learned of her desperate condition, Elijah immediately ordered her to do two hard things: "Don't be afraid," and "First make a small cake of bread for me from what you have and bring it to me" (1 Kings 17:13). He was asking her to give up both her fear and her supper.

Elijah dared to speak so boldly to the widow for two reasons. First, he represented not only his own hunger but also the full authority of God, to whom all things are due. Second, his request was in actuality a test of her potential for faith in the true God. Elijah followed up his demands with a clear promise. "For this is what the LORD, the God of Israel, says: 'The jar of flour will not be used up and the jug of oil will not run dry until the day the LORD gives rain on the land'" (1 Kings 17:14). Would she trust this God enough to give his prophet her last meal before receiving anything but a promise from him in return? Surprisingly, she would and she did.

Today God asks each one of us the same question. Are we willing to surrender to him everything we possess—our fears and ourselves—unconditionally? Or would we hold something back, just in case he does not keep his word and dumps us back in the lap of starvation? If we truly know that we are his sheep, then surely we can rest peacefully in the care of the perfect shepherd (consider John 10).

Since they were already at death's door, one might argue that in giving their last crumb to Elijah the widow and her son did not really have so much to lose. One day more or less did not matter at that point, and any possibility of escape was worth a try. But the key verse of this passage is 1 Kings 17:15: "She went away and did as Elijah had told her." Her simple obedience does not convey such a negative attitude. Rather, she willingly served the prophet, not because she had given up all hope but because she earnestly believed and desired to receive his promise of provision. She was truly desperate, not only for physical nourishment but also for spiritual encouragement.

The widow was not disappointed, for verses 15 and 16 continue: "So there was food every day for Elijah and for the woman and her family. For the jar of flour was not used up and the jug of oil did not run dry, in keeping with the word of the LORD spoken by Elijah."

What could be more pitiful than this scene of a widow gathering two sticks to cook a last meager mouthful for herself and her son? Only at the last possible moment a prophet appeared with a promise of God's abundant blessing, which was fulfilled because the woman believed and obeyed. Then what joy they expressed in their report of God's providing just enough food to sustain all of them each day during the famine!

Admittedly, this story may seem a bit extreme, but perhaps God has preserved it in his Word in order to move us to contemplate both our own greater resources and his great glory, which demands and deserves our total worship and subservience. Surely our situations, however grim, are not as desperate as this poor woman's; yet we, too, can place everything we have in God's hands for his service.

Again, there are two thoughts to consider. First, every asset of which we could boast, either talent or possession, devolves from God by his grace, not from our own merit or achievement. There is nothing we could think of to give to God that did not originate in him as his gift to us. Sharing what we have with others, out of hearts grateful to God the giver, is an act of love and worship (see Matt. 10:42). Rather than pity the widow of

Zarephath, we ought to adopt her attitude of totally yielding to God, even when it appeared to bring her to the very threshold of death. The apostle Paul knew this same secret, since his whole purpose was to serve Christ.

> I have learned to be content whatever the circumstances. I know what it is to be in need, and I know what it is to have plenty. I have learned to be content in any and every situation, whether well fed or hungry, whether living in plenty or in want (Phil. 4:11–12).

In Mark 12:41–44, Jesus praised another widow for contributing just two copper coins, "all she had to live on." Thus we realize that the essence of our sharing is not measured in the amount of the gift but in the attitude of the giver.

The second lesson is derived from the first. If we believe that everything we possess has its origin in God, who provides perfectly for all our needs, then the way we feel about the hospitality we offer to others is really a reflection of our attitude toward God himself. If we don't think that our cooking, our finances, or our guest bedrooms are good enough for inviting people to share them with us, what we are really expressing is our own sense of doubt as to whether God has indeed been good enough to us. If we are truly and humbly thankful for what he has provided, we are freer to share it joyfully, without self-conscious pretense or embarrassment. Having accepted his gifts to us, our offering them to others is an act of praise and worship.

> Offer hospitality to one another without grumbling. Each one should use whatever gift he has received to serve others, faithfully administering God's grace in its various forms. If anyone speaks, he should do it with the strength God provides, so that in all things God may be praised through Jesus Christ. To him be the glory and the power for ever and ever. Amen (1 Peter 4:9–11).

To do otherwise, either by hoarding or by feeling too inadequate to share, is in fact a manifestation of self-pride and doubt in God's ability or interest to care for us in the future. The widow of Zarephath shows us a beautiful model of humble hospitality, while we see God's delight in providing her daily bread (see Matt. 6:11).

## God's Faithfulness

The widow's story does not end with God's miraculous provision during the famine, however, and the sequel has another valuable lesson for us. As with the Shunammite woman, this widow's son became sick and died, causing her to berate Elijah. "What do you have against me, man of God? Did you come to remind me of my sin and kill my son?" (1 Kings 17:18). In her agony of grief she had quickly forgotten her previous experiences of God's goodness, just as we today can so easily lose sight of our blessings when trials come into our lives. Yet God was neither tormenting her nor contradicting himself in dealing with the widow. Instead, he was giving her an opportunity to experience his love in a different way and to deepen her faith when he restored the child to her in answer to Elijah's prayers. In the same way he may allow his children today to experience severe hardships and losses in order to draw us to depend on him more fully. At such times we can find encouragement in the words of Hebrews 12:2–11:

> Let us fix our eyes on Jesus, the author and perfecter of our faith, who for the joy set before him endured the cross, scorning its shame, and sat down at the right hand of the throne of God. Consider him who endured such opposition from sinful men, so that you will not grow weary and lose heart. . . . Endure hardship as discipline; God is treating you as sons. For what son is not disciplined by his father? . . . Our fathers disciplined us for a little while as they thought best; but God disciplines us for our good, that we may share in his holiness. No discipline seems pleasant at the time, but painful. Later on, however, it produces a harvest of righteousness and peace for those who have been trained by it.

In considering the widow of Zarephath, we must keep in mind that she did not enjoy a personal relationship with God such as Elijah knew or such as believers can experience today through the Holy Spirit. Elijah had spoken God's promise to her, and God had fulfilled his word by providing flour and oil each day. But her direct knowledge of God was limited. Her bitter question to Elijah when her son died reveals the relative shallowness of her personal understanding of God's character up to that point. Elijah, however, a true man of God as she had called him, did not flinch at her words. He answered simply, "Give me your son," and carried him to his room

155

alone to pray, "O LORD my God, have you brought tragedy also upon this widow I am staying with, by causing
her son to die? . . . O LORD my God, let this boy's life
return to him" (1 Kings 17:19–21).

Although it is true that not every prayer of this kind is
answered in the way we might wish, Elijah knew God
intimately and trusted both his character and his power.
The Lord heard and responded to this prayer (1 Kings
17:22–23) and thereby permitted the widow to deepen
her understanding of his nature. She continued to relate
to God only through his prophet, but her fears and
doubts were transformed to trust, as reflected in her last
affirmation to Elijah, "Now I know that you are a man of
God and that the word of the LORD from your mouth is
the truth" (1 Kings 17:24).

This certainty was the extra blessing of spiritual encouragement for which God had sent Elijah to Sidon.
The widow of Zarephath, limited in her basic knowledge
of God, her resources, and her personal experience, recognized and responded to the word of the Lord as the
truth. God responded to her weakest gesture of hospitality with his fullest blessing and revelation as provider
and source of life, because he recognized her humble
spirit and open heart.

In the same way humility and openness must charac-
terize the hospitality we extend to others. Jesus said, "If
ye continue in my word, then are ye my disciples indeed;
And ye shall know the truth, and the truth shall make
you free" (John 8:31–32, KJV). Do you affirm the truth of
Christ's presence in your life by freely sharing all that he
is and has given to you? In what ways have you experienced his faithfulness in abundantly providing for your
needs when you turn to him obediently?

# 12

## Deborah, Keturah, and Abishag

### Primary Scripture Readings

Genesis 24:59; 35:8
Genesis 25:1–4
1 Kings 1–2

### Supplementary Reference
Philippians 2:17

### Questions for Study and Discussion

**1.** Read Genesis 24 and 35 to learn about Deborah. Whom did she serve? For how long? Did she come to her position by choice? How well, do you think, did she accommodate herself to the needs of the family?

**2.** How did Rebekah and her family feel about Deborah, do you think? How was Deborah honored for her life of faithful service?

**3.** How old was Abraham at the time Keturah is first mentioned? Do you think she was a member of his household before Sarah's death? Justify your answer. How do you account for Keturah's large family?

**4.** Being an advanced age, what special qualities would Abraham have needed in a wife? Did Keturah expect anything special from him in return, do you think? What did Abraham do for her children? How do you think Keturah felt about his gifts?

**5.** What unique service did Abishag perform for old King David? Why was it necessary? How did Abishag feel about being assigned such a role, do you think?

**6.** How was Abishag involved in a plot to undermine Solomon's kingdom? What did Solomon do about the threat? Do you think Abishag felt protected or thwarted by his actions? Why?

**7.** Each of these three women seemed to have served selflessly and successfully for extended periods of time in special situations. What rights and expectations did they have, do you think? Why did God bother to record their names in his Word? What lessons do you learn from their examples, which might help you to become more aware of needs and more willing to pour yourself out for others (Phil. 2:17)?

In this section on service we need to include several special servants mentioned in the Old Testament. It seems that when we talk of servants today, we are usually deploring the lack of "good help," meaning that we wish the people whom we hire to do our dirty work would be more competent and less complaining about it. The three women we consider in this chapter may help us to raise our sights beyond our selfishness to see the beauty and privilege of service, and may give us the desire to become more excellent servants in the eyes of God.

158

## Deborah

The name Deborah usually calls to mind the heroic judge and leader of the Israelites whose biography is found in Judges 4 and 5. But the Bible mentions another Deborah in a much briefer sketch who may be just as heroic in her own way, and who also offers an important challenge to us. Only two verses, separated by eleven chapters, set down the beginning and the end of her long life of service.

When Rebekah agreed to go with Abraham's servant to become Isaac's wife, Laban's family accepted her decision and blessed her. "So they sent their sister Rebekah on her way, along with her nurse and Abraham's servant and his men" (Gen. 24:59). Genesis 35:8 states, "Now Deborah, Rebekah's nurse, died and was buried under the oak below Bethel. So it was named Allon Bacuth."

Such a record is so brief it seems to be only a trivial detail among the broad, powerful portraits of the patriarchs; but it is worthy of our attention, for a moment at least, if we apply to ourselves this lesson of service. For one thing, very few women in the Bible are recognized to the extent of having their deaths and burials recorded. Rebekah's death, for example, was not mentioned in its chronological sequence, though we find out later that she had been buried at Machpelah (Gen. 49:31). The honor of being officially "gathered to one's fathers" was primarily reserved for men. Women and servants were rarely so recognized, even when their lives were more fully developed in Scripture than Deborah's.

From other sources, we know that the position of nurse was one of importance in ancient times. It was a role that often comprised the function of confidante as well as that of nursemaid, tutor, or guardian. Men also served young princes in this capacity. In our own culture the role of nanny or governess may sound pretentious or old-fashioned to our ears, but in other times and places the position often implied dignity, trust, and growing intimacy. Deborah served Rebekah in this way, and she remained in Isaac's household after the death of her mistress.

How long did Deborah serve? We know that Isaac was forty years old when Rebekah came to be his wife (Gen. 25:20). Genesis 35:28 records his death at age one hundred eighty. Deborah's death is recorded in verse 8 of the same chapter. It is not clear how long a time elapsed between verses 8 and 28, however. In the intervening verses we read of God's renewed covenant at Bethel, Rachel's death in childbirth, and Jacob's residence beyond Migdal Eder. Less than ten years seems a reasonable estimate for the span of these activities. So it is possible that Deborah served Rebekah and remained with Isaac's family for 125 years or more!!

Nothing specific is stated concerning the quality of Deborah's service during such a long period, a fact which is meaningful in itself. In sharp contrast to Hagar, who caused so much upheaval over her servant status under Sarah, Deborah must have served quietly and capably, almost invisibly, throughout her long lifetime. She certainly earned the deep devotion of the entire household, as indicated by the genuine mourning over her death and the naming of the tree Allon Bacuth, which means *the oak of weeping.*

At my home several lawnmowers have demanded constant attention and repair to keep them performing their duties. Meanwhile, the attic fan has functioned efficiently for many years. We can never be sure that we will be able to cut the grass without a breakdown, but we flip the fan switch without giving it a thought. The expression *The squeaky wheel gets the oil* fits our situation very well. But what about the person who quietly does his or her job without complaint or commotion? In the example of Deborah the Bible awards an honorable mention to this quiet, faithful servant and encourages us to persevere in the necessary but unsung jobs we are asked to perform.

How long and how well do you accept the position of quiet, capable servant to others? What level of recognition or appreciation do you expect before you contribute your efforts to a project? How quickly do you break down or give up under pressure? In short, are you a squeaky wheel that demands attention, or one that hums faithfully and efficiently in its appointed groove?

Jesus provided his disciples with both the teaching and the example of service when he washed their feet and explained:

> "You call me 'Teacher' and 'Lord,' and rightly so, for that is what I am. Now that I, your Lord and Teacher, have washed your feet, you also should wash one another's feet. I have set you an example that you should do as I have done for you. I tell you the truth, no

161

> servant is greater than his master, nor is a messenger greater than the one who sent him. Now that you know these things, you will be blessed if you do them" (John 13:13–17).

Such service does not need to be trumpeted proudly nor squeaked loudly with self-pity. Deborah apparently caused no ripple in Isaac's household during all her years of devoted obedience. We see her honored only after her death, not during her lifetime. She continues to serve us as an example of one who does her work, however menial, with selflessness and honor; and she challenges us to re-evaluate our attitudes and actions throughout the long course of our lives. Will there be a tree named in tribute to your lifetime of service?

Even without such an honor on earth we can be confident of God's approval when we follow the example of his Son, who was sent to be the suffering servant in out behalf.

> Your attitude should be the same as that of Christ Jesus:
> Who, being in very nature God, did not consider
> equality with God something to be grasped,
> but made himself nothing, taking the very nature of a servant,
> being made in human likeness.
> And being found in appearance as a man, he humbled himself
> and became obedient to death—even death on a cross!
> (Phil. 2:5–8)

## Keturah and Abishag

Are they places or people, men or women? Although their names may be unfamiliar to us, these faithful servants provided for the special needs of two of God's best friends, Abraham and David, in their old age. In recent years, when care for the elderly has become a critical issue both for the government and for the church as well as for individual families, we should benefit from a brief look at the relationships and attitudes of these women toward the old men for whom they cared.

The descriptions of the two men at the time these women served them are remarkably similar. In the King James Version, Genesis 24 begins thus: "And Abraham was old, and well stricken in age: and the LORD had blessed Abraham in all things." 1 Kings 1 opens with: "Now King David was old and stricken in years. . . ." When we think of David it is usually of the period of his youthful courage and leadership as recorded in 1 and 2 Samuel. It is difficult to imagine him an old man shivering under his blankets. But shiver he did, and God provided a perfect solution in the beautiful form of Abishag.

We do think of Abraham as an old man, because he was already a senior citizen when God called him out of Ur; he and Sarah were both flabbergasted at God's promise of a child yet to come from their ancient bodies. After Sarah died, Abraham seemed even more sure that his own end was near, so he bound his servant by oath to procure a wife for Isaac, doubting that he would live long enough to welcome her.

It is difficult to determine exactly when Keturah joined Abraham's family. She is not mentioned by name until Genesis 25:1: "Abraham took another wife, whose name was Keturah. She bore him Zimran, Jokshan, Medan, Midian, Ishbak and Shuah." If we understand this to

163

mean that Abraham did not marry Keturah until shortly after Isaac's marriage to Rebekah recorded in the preceding chapter, we must calculate that Abraham was at least one hundred forty years old! If it was such a miracle for Abraham to become a father at age one hundred, we might well ask how he managed to sire six more sons forty years later!

Some scholars argue that Keturah must have been one of Abraham's concubines for some time before that, and only became elevated to wife status at this late point in the story. In Hebrew the verb allows the translation of Genesis 25:1 to be *Abraham had taken another wife.* This would have been standard practice in his day, and seems to be supported by the plural nouns in Genesis 25:6: "But while he was still living, he gave gifts to the sons of his concubines and sent them away from his son Isaac to the land of the east." Isaac was clearly the protected child of promise, but it appears that he was not the only male offspring in the household. Against this argument, however, stands the poignant story of Hagar and Ishmael (Gen. 16 and 21), after which experience I believe Sarah would have insisted on Abraham's faithfulness to her marriage bed until her death. When, do you think, did Keturah come to complete God's promise that Abraham would become the "father of many nations" (Gen. 17:4)?

We must be careful not to treat the elderly members of our own families as mentally "out to pasture" or "over the hill" just because they are advanced in years. Abraham, who had worried about his physical condition through nine chapters of Genesis, was apparently more virile at the end of his life than during his first century. King David became old and cold, but his authority and ability to rule were still recognized in spite of his physical weaknesses. Abishag was chosen by David's servants to minister to the special needs brought on by his advanced age, but David remained in firm command of the nation, even surprising his rebellious son Adonijah by his timely appointment of Solomon as heir to the throne.

Both Keturah and Abishag provided comfort to their old men, albeit in different ways. Just as Isaac was comforted after his mother's death by his wife Rebekah (Gen. 24:67), Abraham received comfort from Keturah. We cannot determine her exact age, nor can we be absolutely sure that Abraham was already a widower at the time he married her; but we are told that Keturah was a comfort to her husband. She bore him six children and raised no complaint against him to cause him any distress worthy of record, even when he left everything he had to Isaac and sent all of her family away to the east. She simply accepted the love and provision Abraham offered on his own terms; so, apparently, did her children.

Abishag's service was unique in the biblical record. The New International Version states:

> When King David was old and well advanced in years, he could not keep warm even when they put covers over him. So his servants said to him, "Let us look for a young virgin to attend the king and take care of him. She can lie beside him so that our lord the king may keep warm." Then they searched throughout Israel for a beautiful girl and found Abishag, a Shunammite, and brought her to the king. The girl was very beautiful; she took care of the king and waited on him, but the king had no intimate relations with her (1 Kings 1:1–4).

165

The King James Version uses the phrase *she cherished the king and ministered to him.* Her job required warmth of heart as well as of body. When David's other wives, children, and servants would not or could not satisfy his special need, she provided the necessary comfort with grace and discretion. Later, King Solomon upheld her loyalty by rejecting Adonijah's request to marry her, which was in reality an affront to David's honor and a potential threat to the kingdom.

Will you prayerfully consider whether there is some elderly person in your family, church, or neighborhood to whom you could offer appropriate comfort, remembering when you do that you are serving Christ as you minister to his people? As he said:

> "Then the King will say to those on his right, 'Come, you who are blessed by my Father; take your inheritance, the kingdom prepared for you since the creation of the world. For I was hungry and you gave me something to eat, I was thirsty and you gave me something to drink, I was a stranger and you invited me in, I needed clothes and you clothed me, I was sick and you looked after me, I was in prison and you came to visit me.'
>
> "Then the righteous will answer him, 'Lord, when did we see you hungry and feed you, or thirsty and give you something to drink? When did we see you a stranger and invite you in, or needing clothes and clothe you? When did we see you sick or in prison and go to visit you?'
>
> "The King will reply, 'I tell you the truth, whatever you did for one of the least of these brothers of mine, you did for me'" (Matt. 25:40).

Each one of us needs to be available to God as a helpful and sensitive servant for his friends, whatever their ages and needs. Even the job of "human hot water bottle" may be a position of dignity and satisfaction when it is rendered "as unto the Lord." (Incidentally, hot water bottles are often called *young virgins* in England today, in unconscious tribute to the beautiful Abishag!)

# 13

## Rahab

### Primary Scripture Reading

Joshua 1, 2, and 6

### Supplementary References

Ezra 1, 2
Acts 16
James 2:24–26

### Questions for Study and Discussion

**1.** Why did Joshua send spies to Jericho? Why did they go to Rahab's house? List all the clues to her character and career you can find in Joshua 2. Why would her house have been a good place for the spies to get the information they needed?

**2.** What did Rahab tell the spies about the condition of Canaan? Why? What did she already know about the Israelites and their God? What did she do for the spies? At what personal risk?

**3.** What were Rahab's motives for helping? What do you think of Rahab's lies to the king's officers? Did she have any alternative? What do you think you would have done?

**4.** What did the spies promise Rahab in return for her help? What conditions were put on their promise? What did Joshua say about their obligation? How completely did Rahab fulfill these conditions? How are they similar to God's requirements for salvation today?

**5.** How long did Rahab have to wait for the spies to return (count the indications of elapsed time from Joshua 2–6)? What did she do in the meantime? How are you using the time of waiting for the Lord's return? How successful was Rahab in bringing her entire family into her house for rescue? Can you think of other biblical examples in which inclusion in one's house by faith was a prerequisite to salvation?

**6.** What happened to Rahab and her family when the spies returned to conquer Jericho? Later in her life? How did she change from the beginning of her story to the end? Why is her name included in Christ's genealogy, in Matthew 1, do you think?

**7.** How did James use Rahab's story to demonstrate the importance of action as a component of faith? How does her witness challenge you? What warnings can you draw from Rahab's story? How does she encourage you to worship?

The writer of Hebrews includes her in his gallery of saints: "By *faith* the prostitute Rahab, because she *welcomed* the spies, was not killed with those who were *disobedient*" (Heb. 11:31, italics added) From such high praise of her we can see that Rahab would fit appropriately into practically any of the chapters in our study— women of faith, hospitality, or obedience—and this in spite of her history of prostitution and deception. More than her sins we want to identify Rahab's strength in holding onto God's promises to find fulfillment and salvation for herself and her family. Her story, found primarily in the Book of Joshua, progresses from whoredom to worship.

## Whoredom

What word does your Bible use to describe Rahab in Joshua 2:1? "Then Joshua son of Nun secretly sent two spies from Shittim. 'Go, look over the land,' he said, 'especially Jericho.' So they went and entered the house of a _____ named Rahab and stayed there." The New International Version uses *prostitute* in the blank, with a footnote stating that *innkeeper* might be a valid alternative. The King James Version calls her a *harlot*. *Whore* is a strong word to find in a Bible study guide, but I think it fits the original language quite well. From the Hebrew word *zoonah,* there can be little doubt that Rahab was a member of woman's oldest profession, no matter how eagerly we try to paint her as a genteel lady. There are three reasons this fact is important.

First, Rahab's occupation explains her accessibility to the spies. Her house was part of the city wall, perhaps close to the gate (Josh. 2:5, 7, 15), but the spies probably selected it as much for its advertisement of the business transacted within as for its location in Jericho. We must remember that prostitution was neither illegal nor uncommon in Canaanite society at that time. This is not to say that the spies were looking for a night on the town instead of performing their assignment. Still, a certain amount of confidentiality could be expected in such a place as Rahab's house. Few questions would be asked. Foreigners would be accepted and information could be gathered more readily there than at the more respectable shops in town. It would be an excellent place in which to learn about the land.

Second, we don't have to water down or clean up Scripture by portraying its characters in only the best light at all times. Rahab's personality makes a powerful study *because* there is such a dramatic change in her lifestyle. She seized her opportunities in the only way she knew, but after her commitment and rescue she never returned to her former ways. Her sins were as scarlet, but now she is washed whiter than snow. The contrast is as graphic as possible, even to the point of this prostitute being in the genealogy of Christ (Matt. 1:5). She reminds me of the woman in Luke 7:37–47, in that "her many sins have been forgiven—for she loved much. But he who has been forgiven little loves little."

Third, to be sure, Rahab was a whore in the physical sense of the word. However, we do well to pause for a moment and confront the fact that in the spiritual sense of the term we are guilty of whoredom (unfaithfulness) whenever we allow another person or thing to usurp God's rightful place of first priority in our lives, as he requires in the first commandment.

Repeatedly in the Old Testament God expressed disappointment and anger concerning Israel's unfaithfulness (whoredom) to him. In the Book of Hosea God roundly condemned Israel's whoredom, using the same strong root word that would apply to unfaithfulness in a marriage relationship: "Go, take unto thee a wife of whoredoms and children of whoredoms; for the land hath committed great whoredom, departing from the LORD" (Hos. 1:2, KJV). Hosea's unfaithful wife clearly demonstrated the spiritual adultery the unfaithful Israelites were committing.

172

Christ calls us Christians his bride and therefore we like to think of ourselves as beautiful and pure, all dressed in white, without blemish. It is easy for us to forget our sinfulness and the price Christ paid to redeem us. Christ clothes us in his righteousness and purifies us. That is his gift to us. Without that gift we are all dead in our sins and wholly without hope. Only by his grace are we saved (Eph. 2:1–10). If we will not face the fact that we are sinners—no better than whores—then we negate the necessity of Christ's death as the costly and complete sacrifice to accomplish our redemption (1 John 1:8—2:2).

## Whole Woman

Having faced up to Rahab's identity as a prostitute, let us go on to consider her as a whole person, not just a painted lady. There is ample basis in the text for admiring her tenacious faith, courage, and resourcefulness.

Rahab's faith is expressed in Joshua 2:8–12. Her moving appeal to the spies should encourage us concerning the power of God to reveal himself to nonbelievers even before we have the opportunity to share our personal testimony with them. Consider what Rahab already knew about God:

> Before the spies lay down for the night, she went up on the roof and said to them, "I *know* that the LORD has given this land to you and that a great fear of you has fallen on us, so that all who live in this country are melting in fear because of you. *We have heard* how the LORD dried up the water of the Red Sea for you when

173

you came out of Egypt, and what you did to Sihon and Og, the two kings of the Amorites east of the Jordan, whom you completely destroyed. *When we heard of it, our hearts sank and everyone's courage failed because of you, for the* LORD *your God is God in heaven above and on the earth below* (Josh. 2:8–11, italics added).

It is interesting to note how closely Rahab's words echo Moses' original appeal to the Israelites to hold onto their faith in God and to receive his blessings:

"Acknowledge and take to heart this day that the LORD is God in heaven above and on the earth below. There is no other. Keep his decrees and commands, which I am giving you today, so that it may go well with you and your children after you and that you may live long in the land the LORD your God gives you for all time" (Deut. 4:39–40).

Similarly, Naaman's confession in 2 Kings 5:15, among others, acknowledges the same elements of God's power, uniqueness, and blessing of his people. Would that God's chosen nation had always remained true to his character, commandments, and call to obedience with as much tenacity as those who, though originally cast as outsiders, became grafted into the true branch by faith (see Rom. 11:17–21)! Whether we are part of the root stock or new shoots, let us remember to appreciate the value of the treasure we possess and manifest in our lives the gratitude and joy that should be consistent with God's great gifts. Do we not sometimes take our faith too much for granted?

174

Realizing both what God had already done and what he was about to do for the Israelites, Rahab risked her life to make a crucial commitment. Her own king had heard about the spies' visit to her house and sent messengers demanding that she turn them over to him. Instead, she hid the spies on her roof and lied by saying, "Yes, the men came to me, but I did not know where they had come from. At dusk, when it was time to close the city gate, the men left. I don't know which way they went. Go after them quickly. You may catch up with them" (Josh. 2:4–5). Surely, if the king's officers had searched and found the spies in Rahab's house, she would have been severely punished, possibly killed, for harboring the enemies of her people. Her firm belief that the only hope for deliverance rested in the God of Israel gave her the courage and the resourcefulness to conceal the spies (v. 6), mislead the guards (v. 5), contract for the safety of her family (vv. 12, 13), and later send the men back to Joshua with the favorable report, "The LORD has surely given the whole land into our hands; all the people are melting in fear because of us" (Josh. 2:24).

Rounding out our impression of Rahab as a whole woman, we find indications of another career in the piles of flax spread to dry on her rooftop where she hid the spies (Josh. 2:6). The rope by which the men escaped from Jericho (2:15) and the scarlet cord with which Rahab was to mark her window when they returned to rescue her (2:18) might have been some of her own handiwork as a spinner and dyer. Without sidestepping her prostitution, we must credit Rahab with the possibility of running a wholesome enterprise, as well.

## Welcome

Rahab welcomed and hid the spies for several reasons. First, it was dictated by the nature of her trade. Prostitutes don't usually turn away the men who come to their doors. Second, it was consistent with her culture's code of hospitality. Because the Israelite spies had come under her roof, Rahab was obligated to protect them at any cost. The same code of hospitality also remains a point of honor in the Middle East today. For Rahab hospitality even took precedence over honesty, for she knowingly lied to the king's messengers in order to save the spies.

Does Rahab's example prove that God condones deceit? Is lying ever justified, or can noble motives change the color of a lie from black to white? Are there degrees of truth? Of course not. Our holy God demands wholly righteous conduct from his people. We must have enough faith to believe that he can accomplish his will without our resorting to immoral behavior to help him out. Rahab's lie was as sinful as her prostitution. But these acts occurred *before* her commitment of faith; after her rescue we see a changed person. She remained "among the Israelites to this day" (Josh. 6:25). She married Salmon and became the mother of Boaz, who married Ruth. The lesson we need to learn from Rahab is not that sin is condoned but that our sin will be purged if we accept by faith the atoning sacrifice of Jesus Christ. Our former lives may have to be put away; but we need not and must not carry the guilt of our past, which has been forgiven, into our new life. Rather than wallow in our unworthiness, let us rejoice in our unmerited redemption.

Concern for her own security was undoubtedly another motive for Rahab's hospitality. Perhaps she identified the spies as Israelites by their language or clothing when they first entered her house. Perhaps she even caught sight of them from her window on the city wall and guessed at their mission while they were still afar off. We do know that for some reason Rahab had already hidden the spies before the arrival of the officers. The verb tenses in Joshua 2:4–7 make this clear: "But the woman *had taken* the two men and hidden them. . . . (But she *had taken* them up to the roof and hidden them under the stalks of flax she had laid out on the roof)" (italics added).

Being a woman of the world, Rahab was skilled at recognizing and seizing an opportunity when it came to her door, rarely losing by any bargain she made. What was it that made her so desperate to protect the spies? Following her affirmation of God's power, of which she had heard and was afraid, Rahab pleaded her case.

"Now then, please swear to me by the LORD that you will show kindness to my family, because I have shown kindness to you. Give me a sure sign that you will spare the lives of my father and mother, my brothers and sisters, and all who belong to them, and that you will save us from death" (Josh. 2:12–13).

Thus, Rahab welcomed the spies in order to save herself and her family.

Today we know that Christians are not to have ulterior motives when we offer hospitality. It should be a pure expression of our love for God, without contingencies or expectations of reward (see Luke 14:12–14). Nevertheless, we must appreciate the fact that Rahab desired to align herself with the Lord's cause and people, for whatever reasons. The spies' response "Our lives for your lives!" (Josh. 2:14) shows us a beautifully positive variation of the traditional code for revenge expressed in Deuteronomy 19:21.

## Witness

Once Rahab had allied herself with the Israelites she immediately became intensely concerned for the safety of her whole family. The spies' promise, in response to her plea, included three conditions: 1) She was not to reveal their intentions (Josh. 2:14, 20); 2) she was to tie the scarlet cord in the window (v. 18); and 3) she was to bring her entire family into her house (vv. 18–19). Otherwise, the Israelites would be released from their oath of protection.

This theme of inclusion in one's house is an important principle in Scripture. Each one of us is accountable to make a personal choice to believe in God, and when we do we become witness to the truth, the joy, and the urgency of his call. People close to us may be influenced to choose or reject the opportunity for salvation. In Genesis 6 and 7, all in Noah's family were saved because they believed and obeyed his order to enter the ark with him. The rest of humanity perished. By contrast, Lot was unable to convince his sons-in-law to leave Sodom, and his

178

wife could not resist taking one backward glance against his orders. They refused to take his witness seriously and so lost their chance for deliverance (Gen. 19). In Exodus 12 the decisive issue was once again the personal choice through faith, not national origin. Every person who took refuge in a house marked with the blood of a lamb escaped God's judgment by the plague of death to the firstborn son. The eldest son of any Israelite who did not come under a marked doorpost perished, while any foreigner who did choose to enter was spared and included in the exodus from Egypt. And again, nearly one thousand years later—after the exile—many outsiders chose to join the remnant of Judah in its return to Jerusalem, while the majority of Jews opted to remain in the relative comfort of Persia (Ezra 1—2).

How successful was Rahab in convincing her relatives to join her and share the salvation of the Lord? The requirements were clear, as was the response of her family. When Joshua sent the spies to fulfill their commitment to her, they

> went in and brought out Rahab, *her father and mother and brothers and all who belonged to her.* They brought out *her entire family* and put them in a place outside the camp of Israel. Then they burned the whole city and everything in it, but they put the silver and gold and the articles of bronze and iron into the treasury of the LORD's house. But Joshua spared Rahab the prostitute, *with her family and all who belonged to her,* because she hid the men Joshua had sent as spies to Jericho—and she lives among the Israelites to this day (Josh. 6:23–25, italics added).

Rahab succeeded in bringing *every* member of her family into her house, and *all* were saved. The rest of the city was destroyed. Thus, Joshua honored the spies' oath. God's hand of protection was also on Rahab more directly. The collapse of the city wall, of which her house was a part, apparently did no harm to the obedient family who remained within.

In the New Testament we find a similar story of inclusion in Acts 16, when the Philippian jailer fell trembling before Paul and Silas after the earthquake and asked,

> "Men, what must I do to be saved?" They replied, "Believe in the Lord Jesus, and you will be saved—*you and your household.*" Then they spoke the word of the Lord *to him and to all the others in his house.* At that hour of the night the jailer took them and washed their wounds; then immediately *he and all his family* were baptized. The jailer brought them into his house and set a meal before them, and *the whole family was filled with joy, because they had come to believe in God* (Acts 16:30–34).

This family was saved not beause of the jailer's faith alone but because they, too, came to believe in God. First Corinthians 7 teaches that an unbelieving spouse is *sanctified* through the presence of the believing spouse, until such time as he or she may be *saved* through personal faith. It is the Holy Spirit who moves within a person's heart, enabling him or her to make that choice. Our task is to affirm the necessity and the blessing of our own commitment to God, and to invite others to be included in the house for salvation with us. Rahab's witness to her family was 100 percent fruitful.

Rahab's witness also serves as a challenge to us. We see her concern and her success in bringing every member of her family into her house for deliverance. Are we so sure of the destruction that results from rejecting God's offer of salvation that we show the same concern in regard to our own families, friends, and neighbors—with the result that others come inside through our witness? Is our faith so strong that it compels us to grab hold of God's promises, even at the price of great personal risk; and is it deep enough to effect drastic and permanent changes in our lifestyles? The apostle James chose Rahab as a powerful illustration of the relationship between what we believe and what we do.

> You see that a person is justified by what he does and not by faith alone. In the same way, was not even Rahab the prostitute considered righteous for what she did when she gave lodging to the spies and sent them in a different direction? As the body without the spirit is dead, so faith without deeds is dead (James 2:24–26).

Do you manifest your faith with bold, unequivocal actions as Rahab did?

Finally, we have considered Rahab's scarlet sins, but let us also notice her scarlet cord by which she marked her window for the spies to return and rescue her (Josh. 2:18). The cord may be seen as a picture of the blood sacrificed for the identification and salvation of Israel at the first Passover, when Moses commanded:

> "Take a bunch of hyssop, dip it into the blood in the basin and put some of the blood on the top and on both

181

sides of the doorframe. Not one of you shall go out the door of his house until morning. When the LORD goes through the land to strike down the Egyptians, he will see the blood on the top and sides of the doorframe and will pass over that doorway, and he will not permit the destroyer to enter your houses and strike you down" (Exod. 12:22–23).

Similarly, Christ's death was the utter fulfillment of God's holy requirement for the blood of an unblemished lamb to be shed in atonement for sin. "Without the shedding of blood there is no forgiveness" (Heb. 9:22). Had Rahab refused to mark her window there would have been no deliverance. How is your life identified with the blood of Christ, who alone can deliver you from sin?

## ✳ Waiting

Even when Rahab made her commitment of faith, rescue was not immediate. The spies did not disappear around the bend and return in a flash with the whole army. How long did she have to wait? Joshua 2—6 gives several indications of how much time elapsed:

1. When they left, they went into the hills and stayed there *three days*. . . . Then the two men started back. They went down out of the hills, forded the river and came to Joshua. . . . (Josh. 2:22–23).
2. *Early in the morning* Joshua and all the Israelites set out from Shittim and went to the Jordan. . . . *After three days* the officers went. . . . (Josh. 3:1–2).

3. . . . take up twelve stones from the middle of the Jordan. . . and put them down at the place where you *stay tonight* (Josh. 4:3).
4. On the *tenth day of the first month* the people went up from the Jordan and camped. . . (Josh. 4:19).
5. And after the whole nation had been circumcised, they remained where they were in camp *until they were healed* (Josh. 5:8).
6. On the evening of *the fourteenth day of the month, . . .* the Israelites celebrated the Passover. *The day after the Passover,* that very day, they ate some of the produce of the land (Josh. 5:10–11).
7. . . . they marched around the city once and returned to the camp. They did this for *six days. On the seventh day,* they got up at daybreak and marched around the city seven times in the same manner, except that on that day they circled the city seven times. The seventh time around, when the priests sounded the trumpet blast, Joshua commanded the people, "Shout! For the LORD has given you the city! The city and all that is in it are to be devoted to the LORD. Only Rahab the prostitute and all who are with her in her house shall be spared, because she hid the spies we sent" (Josh. 6:14–17, italics added).

By calculating the above time references we estimate that Rahab had to wait at least twenty-four days, or more than three weeks, before she had any confirmation that the spies had remembered her or that Joshua would honor their promise. Did she lose courage or conviction during those weeks of uncertainty? Did she begin to think that she had only imagined the danger and dread of the Lord that had prompted her to hide the spies? Did she feel embarrassed or doubtful when nothing happened after she had spread the word to her family, so that little by little they got tired of waiting and went back to their normal routines? Clearly not. When the young men went into her house, they brought out her entire family (Josh. 6:23). They were all there; none had given up the vigil, because Rahab never let go of her confidence in God's promise as their only hope.

How good a "waiter" are you? When the walls of the world's security come tumbling down around you, or even when nothing seems to be happening for either good or bad (Zeph. 1:12), or when you feel forgotten, rejected, or dejected (O Lord, how long?), can you persevere with confidence? "Be still before the LORD and wait patiently for him" (Ps. 37:7).

Rahab waited weeks. Perhaps you have already waited years to be rescued from your distress. God does not guarantee immediate deliverance from your circumstances, but he does promise to be with you *in* them, and to strengthen you with his presence *through* them if you continue to trust his perfect care and timing. While you wait *for* him make it your first desire to wait *on* him.

## Warnings

Before concluding with the beautiful lessons on worship let us summarize some of the warnings to be found in Rahab's story. We have agreed to accept biblical personalities as whole people, without whitewashing their sins. Christ's human genealogy consists of real human beings, not phony saints, and Rahab's presence on the roster is an important reminder to us that God is more interested in the progress of personal faith than in any

184

outward pose of perfection. Since only God can know each heart (1 Sam. 16:7), it is not our right to stand in judgment of one whom God has redeemed.

Rahab negotiated to get the spies to agree, "Our lives for your lives!" (Josh. 2:14). They accepted her terms with a few conditions, as we have seen. But we must not point to her example to justify our bargaining with God. His standards of righteousness are clearly set forth in his Word, and we cannot count on any last-minute tradeoffs to secure our salvation. Either we belong to Christ or we are lost. Rahab's conversion was not the final event of her life, but the beginning of a new life of faith and obedience. There is no blessing to be gained from sin, even though the abundance of God's grace brings forgiveness and adds to his glory (Rom. 3:5–8).

Another warning from Rahab's story is the observation that we are still in enemy territory. She and her family were not taken to the safety of the Israelite camp before the destruction of Jericho commenced. When the walls crumbled, there they were in the midst of them, suffering the noise and dust, the danger of falling rocks, and the terror along with the rest of the city's residents. We, too, are still part of the world, though we are not to be worldly. The day of the Lord will be terrifying as well as triumphant, gory as well as glorious, as the prophets have described. Believers in Christ might not escape without pain, even though we can be confident of our ultimate reunion with our Lord, which he has promised (John 14:3). We, too, must count the cost as we recognize the truth and the urgency of God's Word.

> Therefore, brothers, since we have confidence to enter the Most Holy Place by the blood of Jesus, by a new

and living way opened for us through the curtain, that is, his body, and since we have a great priest over the house of God, *let us* draw near to God with a sincere heart in full assurance of faith, having our hearts sprinkled to cleanse us from a guilty conscience and having our bodies washed with pure water. *Let us* hold unswervingly to the hope we profess, for he who promised is faithful. And *let us* consider how we may spur one another on toward love and good deeds. *Let us* not give up meeting together, as some are in the habit of doing, but *let us* encourage one another—and all the more as you see the Day approaching (Heb. 10:19–25, italics added).

Let us, let us, let us, let us, let us!!

We must do more than admire Rahab for her faith and obedience, her patience and her courage. Each one of us must choose, and act upon our choices as well. Moses presented the options for life or death in Deuteronomy 30 and 31. Joshua renewed the covenant between God and Israel at the end of his book:

"Now fear the LORD and serve him with all faithfulness. Throw away the gods your forefathers worshiped beyond the River and in Egypt, and serve the LORD. But if serving the LORD seems undesirable to you, then choose for yourselves this day whom you will serve, whether the gods your forefathers served beyond the River or the gods of the Amorites, in whose land you are living. But as for me and my household, we will serve the LORD."

Then the people answered, "Far be it from us to forsake the LORD to serve other gods! . . . We too will serve the LORD, because he is our God."

Joshua said to the people, "You are not able to serve the LORD. He is a holy God; he is a jealous God. He will not forgive your rebellion and your sins. If you forsake the LORD and serve foreign gods, he will turn and bring disaster on you and make an end of you, after he has been good to you."

But the people said to Joshua, "No! We will serve the LORD."

Then Joshua said, "You are witnesses against yourselves that you have chosen to serve the LORD."

. . . And the people said to Joshua, "We will serve the LORD our God and obey him (Josh. 24:14–24).

Would you add your voice to this commitment and covenant?

## Worship

Worship of God is any act of a creature intended to acknowledge and honor its Creator. It may be formal or informal, spontaneous or structured, individual or corporate in expression. It may last only a moment, but it should be repeated over and over again during a lifetime. How does Rahab's life lead us to worship?

First, her decision to hide the spies because of what she knew about the God of Israel was an act of worship. She worshiped God when she witnessed to her family. She continued worshiping with the Israelites from the time of her deliverance "to this day." She married Salmon, a prince of Judah; her son was Boaz; her grandson was Obed, whose name means *worship* or *service.*

We, too, can worship God through our study of Rahab. We gain a special understanding of his character

187

as we see him dealing with such a woman and with us. We recognize his intimate knowledge of our sinfulness and our need for salvation. We see his power and his desire to redeem every soul that turns to him in faith. We discover his justice and his merciful love even inside Jericho, which had to be destroyed because of its sins. And we find that the only prerequisite for God's guarantee of deliverance is that we must be "in the house." "And we are his house, if we hold on to our courage and the hope of which we boast" (Heb. 3:6). What a glorious testimony to God's holiness, his power, his faithfulness, and his salvation! Rahab welcomed the spies and her whole family into her house. Will you join them in God's house, as his house, by faith?